LAW
ENFORCEMENT
AGENCIES

BOMB SQUAD

LAW ENFORCEMENT AGENCIES

Bomb Squad

Border Patrol

Federal Bureau of Investigation

The Secret Service

SWAT Teams

The Texas Rangers

LAW
ENFORCEMENT
A G E N C I E S

BOMB SQUAD

Michael Newton

CHELSEA HOUSE
P U B L I S H E R S
An imprint of Infobase Publishing

BOMB SQUAD

Chelsea House
An imprint of Infobase Publishing
132 West 31st Street
New York NY 10001

Library of Congress Cataloging-in-Publication Data

Newton, Michael, 1951-
Bomb squad / Michael Newton.
p. cm. — (Law enforcement agencies)
Includes bibliographical references and index.
ISBN-13: 978-1-60413-624-1 (hardcover : alk. paper)
ISBN-10: 1-60413-624-3 (hardcover : alk. paper) 1. Bomb squads.
2. Explosives—Detection. 3. Bombings—Prevention. 4. Explosives—
Safety measures. 5. Terrorism—Prevention. I. Title. II. Series.

HV8080.B5N49 2010   363.17′98—dc22

Chelsea House books are available at special discounts when purchased
in bulk quantities for businesses, associations, institutions,
or sales promotions. Please call our Special Sales Department
in New York at (212) 967-8800 or (800) 322-8755.

You can find Chelsea House on the World Wide Web at http://www.chelseahouse.com

Text design and composition by Erika K. Arroyo
Cover design by Keith Trego
Cover printed by Bang Printing, Brainerd, Minn.
Book printed and bound by Bang Printing, Brainerd, Minn.
Date printed: November 2010

Printed in the United States of America

10 9 8 7 6 5 4 3 2 1

This book is printed on acid-free paper.

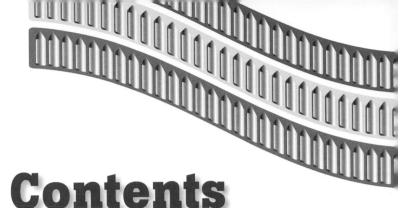

Contents

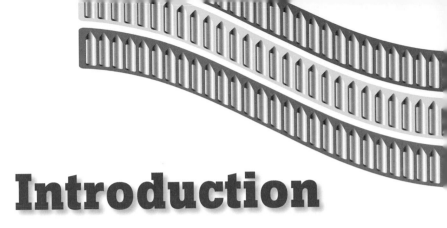

Introduction

Explosives have played a large part in the creation of the modern world. Some fear that explosives may destroy it, either accidentally or through the actions of malicious human beings. Even if those fears prove baseless, wars and global terrorism guarantee that bombs and their ingredients affect quality of life each day.

In 1996 former U.S. Navy Commander Harlan Ullman and ex-Deputy Assistant Secretary of Defense James Wade published a paper on warfare declaring that massive force—including nuclear cruise missiles and laser-guided "smart bombs"—should be used in future conflicts "to affect the will, perception, and understanding of the adversary to fit or respond to our strategic policy ends through imposing a regime of Shock and Awe."[1] Seven years later, President George W. Bush and Secretary of Defense Donald Rumsfeld used the same phrase to describe America's invasion of Iraq.

Sadly, that application of "shock and awe" did not produce the desired result. As this book went to press the war continued, claiming more lives every day.

Modern theorists, of course, did not invent "shock and awe." Attila the Hun's cavalry achieved the same effect as it swept across Europe in A.D. 451–52, while Adolf Hitler's *blitzkrieg* ("lightning war") conquered eight European nations and the western part of Russia during 1939–41. Between those dates, explosives made the difference.

The first known use of explosive or incendiary (fire-setting) weapons involved "Greek fire," introduced in A.D. 668. Chinese alchemists discovered gunpowder in the ninth century, while pursuing the secret of immortality, and their military successors published the first recipe for making it in 1044. By 1259, residents of Qingzhou were manufacturing a thousand iron-cased bombs per month, on average.[2] Meanwhile, China's deadly secret had spread throughout Europe and the Muslim world. British priest and philosopher Roger Bacon (1214–94) was the first to publish a European recipe for gunpowder, in his *Opus Majus* of 1267.

There would be no turning back.

English philosopher Roger Bacon was a key figure in the spread of knowledge of gunpowder in Europe. *(Hulton-Deutsch Collection/ Corbis)*

Hungarian engineers pioneered black-powder blasting of rock in 1627, and German miners carried the practice to Britain's Cornish tin mines in 1670. America's first black powder mill was built at Milton, Massachusetts, in 1675. Benjamin Franklin compressed black powder into firearms cartridges in 1750. Eighty years later, New York inventor Moses Shaw designed a technique for setting off explosives with electric sparks. The following year, 1831, Britain's William Bickford invented the first safety fuse. Italian chemist Ascanio Sobrero discovered nitro glycerine in 1846, while German scientist Joseph Wilbrand created trinitrotoluene (TNT) in 1863. Alfred Nobel, a Swede (for whom the Nobel Prize is named), invented the first blasting cap in 1864, stabilized nitroglycerine with other chemicals to create dynamite in 1866, and created "gelignite" (the first plastic explosive) in 1875.[3]

Aside from use in warfare, broadened to include Earth-shattering nuclear weapons after 1945, explosives are widely used in construction and mining, to clear land for farming, to extinguish burning oil wells, and for many other beneficial purposes.

And they are also used by criminals to kill, maim, or intimidate, and as a tool for robbery of banks, safes, warehouses—anyplace, in short, where massive concentrated force may be required. Terrorists first used explosives in 1605, in a bungled plot to assassinate England's King James I and destroy the Houses of Parliament. Anti-Catholic rioters destroyed a Charlestown, Massachusetts, convent with crude firebombs in 1834, while Irish nationalists bombed British targets in the 1880s. "Black Hand" extortion gangs—disorganized forerunners of America's national crime syndicate—used dynamite to terrorize Italian immigrants in the late 19th and early 20th centuries. White racists set off hundreds of bombs to protest the advance of civil rights for African Americans between 1947 and 1972. Beginning in the 1960s, radical opponents of the war in Vietnam bombed corporate and military targets nationwide. "Pro-life" extremists carried the war to women's clinics in the 1980s, and later "patriot militias" attacked government buildings—including Oklahoma City's Alfred P. Murrah Federal Building, where a truck bomb killed 168 victims in April 1995. After the terrorist attacks of September 11, 2001, fear of further attacks by Muslim fanatics spread. Fears were heightened by terrorists such as Richard Reid,

A bomb squad officer inspects an SUV in New York's Times Square on May 2, 2010, after a potentially powerful bomb was found inside of it. Faisal Shahzad, the man responsible for building the bomb and parking the vehicle in Times Square, was arrested two days after the bomb was discovered. *(Associated Press)*

the shoe bomber, who tried to detonate explosives hidden in his shoes on American Airlines Flight 63 on December 22, 2001. However, even as bombing threats took on a more international scope, homegrown gangsters and bigots were still armed and dangerous.

According to the U.S. Bomb Data Center, operated by the Bureau of Alcohol, Tobacco, Firearms and Explosives (ATF), American police recorded 3,445 explosives incidents in 2006, which includes successful or attempted bombings and firebombings, stolen explosives, and other categories. Those attacks killed 14 persons and injured 135, while ATF agents referred 745 cases for criminal prosecution in federal court.[4]

That onslaught of violence, with its vast potential for destruction, requires a special response from law enforcement. *Bomb Squad* examines the history of that response, the techniques used to locate and disarm explosives, and the risks involved for officers who face death or disfigurement each time they respond to a bomb threat.

Chapter 1, "Explosives," examines the different kinds of explosives used by criminals, and the broad role of law enforcement in combating bombers.

Chapter 2, "Bombing," surveys the history of criminal bombings from 1605 to the present day, paralleled by the evolution of police teams and programs designed to ensure public safety.

Chapter 3, "Underworld Bombing," reviews the use of explosives by organized crime in America and around the world, including global "narcoterrorism" and the campaigns to suppress it.

Chapter 4, "Mail Bombs," explores the use of letter and parcel bombs from 1764 to the 21st century, coupled with techniques developed by U.S. postal inspectors and other authorities to keep deadly packages out of the mail.

Chapter 5, "Bomb Squad Fatalities," presents case histories of bomb squad officers and other law enforcement personnel slain by bombers, with examination of protective gear used to safeguard them.

Chapter 6, "Explosives Detection," presents the various tools and techniques used by modern crime fighters to discover bombs and illegal stockpiles of explosives.

Chapter 7, "Rendered Safe," describes the process from discovery of bombs to their deactivation and disposal, including methods used to trace and identify bombers.

Chapter 8, "Loose Nukes," confronts the ultimate nightmare of nuclear weapons in criminal hands and the systems in place to prevent instant mass-murder.

Explosives

Black Tom Island, New Jersey

Black Tom Island was a speck of land in New York Harbor, near Liberty Island, until 1880, when engineers built a causeway and railroad line connecting it to the Jersey City waterfront. Used thereafter as a shipping depot, Black Tom expanded in 1905 in the form of landfill dumped by the Lehigh Valley Railroad Company. Its mile-long pier supported warehouses of the National Dock and Storage Company.

By 1915, as World War I raged in Europe and British warships blocked ships of the rival Central Powers from access to America's Eastern Seaboard, Black Tom had become an offshore storehouse for explosives, including some 2 million pounds of ammunition packed in railroad freight cars. On July 29, 1916, a barge bearing 100,000 pounds of TNT was moored at Black Tom Island, awaiting escort to Britain for use in the war.

Shortly after midnight on July 30, Black Tom's security guards noted several fires on the pier. Some guards fled, while others stayed to battle the flames. By the time Jersey City firefighters arrived, the blaze was out of control. At 2:08 A.M. the TNT barge exploded, causing $100,000 in damage to the nearby Statue of Liberty, and shattering windows from Jersey City to Manhattan's Times Square. Shock waves from the blast were felt in Philadelphia and Maryland. Surprisingly, though hundreds of persons were injured, police confirmed only seven deaths.[1]

Firefighters try to quench the flames after the allied munitions plant on Black Tom Island exploded on July 29, 1916. *(Bettmann/ Corbis)*

While no one was arrested for the Black Tom explosion, authorities called it an act of sabotage, allegedly directed by Germany's ambassador to the United States, Johann Heinrich von Bernstorff. The only suspect named in print was Michael Kristoff, an Eastern European immigrant who lived with relatives in Bayonne, New Jersey, until his death in 1928. Kristoff had served in the U.S. Army, but rumors claimed that he was paid $500 to set the fires on Black Tom's pier. Thirteen years after the blast, on the eve of World War II, a German-American Mixed Claims Commission officially blamed Germany for sabotage at Black Tom. In 1953 diplomats fixed a $50 million price tag on the damage. Germany made the final payment in 1979.

GOING "BOOM!"

Cartoonist Scott Adams, creator of the *Dilbert* comic strip, once said, "There are very few personal problems that cannot be solved through a suitable application of high explosives."[2] But what exactly *are* explosives?

Technically speaking, an explosion is any sudden release of energy and expanse of volume, usually accompanied by high temperatures and release of gases, creating a physical shock wave. Scientists recognize six types of explosives on Earth.

- *Natural* explosions, such as those produced by volcanic action or other spontaneous ignition of natural gases, are produced by nature.
- *Vapor* explosions are produced by the gaseous expansion of boiling liquids within a confined space, such as a boiler.
- *Electrical* explosions are high-voltage faults that melt insulating materials and some metals, causing fires.
- *Magnetic* explosions are created on rare occasions by excessive pressure within an electromagnet.
- *Chemical* explosions normally involve a rapid and violent oxidation reaction that produces large amounts of hot gas.
- *Nuclear* explosions draw their destructive power either from fission (splitting the nucleus of an atom) or from a combination of fission and *fusion* (the merging of atomic nuclei).

All explosions are destructive, and while some—vapor, electrical, or magnetic—may result from deliberate sabotage of machines or other equipment, they are not classified as bombs—devices specifically built to produce an explosion.

Experts differentiate between military and civilian bombs. The first group, mass-produced for use in warfare, is also called ordnance or munitions, including aerial bombs (dropped from planes), rockets and missiles, mines, grenades, and artillery shells. Unexploded ordnance (UXOs) or unexploded bombs (UXBs) are often found on battlefields, requiring special teams to remove and disarm them.

Civilian bombs are generally custom-made for a specific purpose or target, produced by bomb-makers with varying levels of skill. Many fail to explode, while others detonate unexpectedly, thanks to faulty construction or timing devices. Bomb squad experts commonly refer to civilian bombs as improvised explosive devices (IEDs), and divide

The triggering mechanisms for improvised explosive devices (IEDs) come in a variety of forms. Cordless phones are common because they are often very powerful, allowing a signal to be transmitted up to a mile or more. *(Ed Darack/Science Faction/Corbis)*

them into three broad categories. Type 1 includes all IEDs carried and placed in position by hand, regardless of size. Type 2 are IEDs worn on the body, either by suicide bombers or selected victims, which have included animals such as dogs, donkeys, and horses. Type 3 includes all vehicle-borne explosive devices (VBIEDs), which may serve either as stationary or self-propelled bombs.

CHOOSING WEAPONS

Bombers, whether military or civilian, choose explosives and construct devices for specific tasks. Some bombs are designed to damage property, either with the initial explosion or fire, while others— antipersonnel devices—are meant to kill or wound people. Antipersonnel devices normally use shrapnel, named for British Major-General Henry Shrapnel (1761–1842), who pioneered development of artillery shells packed with lead musket balls. Shrapnel in modern military ordnance takes many forms, from shell-casing fragments to flechettes (metal darts stabilized by tailfins). Shrapnel in IEDs may include any objects readily available, ranging from glass marbles, nails, and scrap metal to ball bearings and lead fishing sinkers.

Chemical explosives are broadly classified as low or high explosives in accordance with their speed of decomposition. Low explosives deflagrate (burn swiftly), whereas high explosives detonate (creating a high-speed shock wave). Most low explosives are mixtures (combining an oxidant and a combustible fuel), while most high explosives are compounds (two or more elements bonded together in a fixed mass).

Common low explosives include gunpowder, various pyrotechnics (fireworks), and devices such as flares, made to briefly illuminate dark places. Their decomposition rate ranges from a few inches per second to roughly 400 meters (1,300 feet) per second.[3] They include the following:

- *Black powder*, a mixture of charcoal, saltpeter (potassium nitrate), and sulfur, used as a propellant in firearms and as the pyrotechnic ("brilliant") element in some fireworks
- *Smokeless powder*, gunpowder modified in the late 19th century by removing sulfur, which reduced the smoke from gunshots and artillery fire
- *Flash powder*, a mixture of a metallic fuel (usually powdered aluminum or magnesium) and an oxidizer (commonly potassium

(Continues on page 20)

FEDERAL EXPLOSIVES CONTROL STATUTE (1970)

In response to acts of terrorism committed during the 1960s, Congress passed a Federal Explosives Control Statute in October 1970. The new law—Title 18 of the U.S. Code, Chapter 40—imposes stiff penalties for misuse of explosive materials. As detailed in Sections 842 and 844, those crimes and penalties include the following:

1. Ten years and/or a $10,000 fine for anyone who receives or transports explosives between states or foreign countries with knowledge that they will be used to kill, injure, or intimidate any person or illegally damage any building, vehicle, or other property. Penalties increase to 20 years and $20,000 if a bombing victim is injured. If deaths result, penalties increase to life imprisonment or death.

2. Ten years in prison and/or a $10,000 fine for anyone who uses explosives or fire to destroy or damage any building, vehicle, or other property owned or used by an agency of the U.S. government or used in interstate commerce. If injuries occur, penalties increase to 20 years and $20,000. In the case of fatalities, convicted defendants face life imprisonment or death.

3. Five years in prison for use of explosives or fire during commission of a felony. The penalty increases to 10 years for a second offense and any thereafter.

4. Five years in prison and/or a $5,000 fine for anyone who uses the mail, a telephone, telegraph, or other "instrument of commerce" (including e-mail) to make a false bomb threat.

5. Five years in prison and/or an unspecified fine for anyone found with illegal explosives at a public airport.

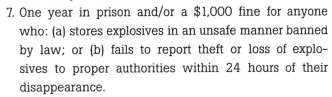

6. Ten years in prison and/or a $10,000 fine for anyone who: (a) imports, manufactures, or sells explosives without proper licenses; (b) withholds information or offers false information to obtain permits for importation, manufacture, or sale of explosives; (c) illegally transports, ships, or receives explosives between states or countries; (d) delivers explosives to any unlicensed person across state lines; (e) delivers explosives to any person whom the supplier believes may illegally transport them across state lines; (f) delivers explosives to any person banned by law from possessing them, including persons under 21 years of age, convicted felons, persons under felony indictment, fugitives from justice, or adjudicated mental defectives; (g) delivers explosives to residents of any state where their possession is banned by law; (h) fails to keep mandatory records of explosives imported, received, manufactured, or sold; (i) falsifies records of explosive imports, receipts, manufacture, or sales; (j) receives, conceals, transports, sells, or distributes stolen explosives; or (k) receives, ships, or transports explosives while under felony indictment, while a fugitive from justice, while illegally using controlled substances, or while adjudicated as a mental defective.

7. One year in prison and/or a $1,000 fine for anyone who: (a) stores explosives in an unsafe manner banned by law; or (b) fails to report theft or loss of explosives to proper authorities within 24 hours of their disappearance.

8. Seizure and forfeiture of any explosive materials used or intended for use in any criminal activity, including unsafe storage as described above.

(Continued from page 17)

chlorate or potassium perchlorate), which produces the loud sound of firecrackers, cherry bombs, and similar noise-making fireworks

- *Amonal,* an explosive mixture of ammonium nitrate, TNT, and powdered aluminum, introduced in 1915 as the chief component of British landmines
- *Armstrong's mixture,* named for British inventor William George Armstrong (1810–1900), a sensitive primary explosive consisting of red phosphorus, potassium chlorate, sulfur, and calcium carbonate, found in the small paper caps sold for toy cap guns
- *Sprengel explosives,* invented by German chemist Hermann Sprengel (1834–1906) in 1873, now referring to a generic group of explosives including any strong oxidizer and a highly reactive fuel, commonly various chlorates and nitroaromatics
- *Cheddites,* closely related to Sprengel explosives and named for the French town of Chedde, where they were manufactured in the early 20th century; consisted of inorganic chlorates, mixed with nitroaromatics and castor oil or paraffin, primarily for use in stone quarries; used chiefly in the *primers* (caps, tubes, or wafers containing percussion powder or compounds used to ignite an explosive charge) of shotgun shells since the 1970s
- *ANFO* (ammonium nitrate and fuel oil), a tertiary explosive commonly used in mines and stone quarries; accidental explosions killed 567 people at Texas City, Texas, in April 1947, and up to 3,000 were killed and injured at Ryongchŏn, North Korea, in April 2004, when two trains carrying liquefied gas and petrol collided; April 1995 also witnessed the ANFO bombing of Oklahoma City's federal building, killing 168 victims and injuring more than 800[4]
- *Oxyliquits,* cheap and easily made explosives that combine liquid oxygen with various organic materials, commonly including carbon, wood meal, or sponge, sometimes with aluminum powder added
- *Panclastites,* explosives similar to oxyliquits, invented by French chemist Eugene Turpin in 1881; created by mixing liquid dinitrogen tetroxide (a component of rocket fuel, also called nitrogen

dioxide) with fuels that may include gasoline, carbon disulfide, nitrotoluene, nitromethane, or a halocarbon

High explosives, by contrast, are much more destructive, detonating at rates between 1,000 meters (3,250 feet) to 9,000 meters (29,250 feet) per second.[5] They are further divided into primary, secondary, and tertiary explosives. Primary explosives, such as nitroglycerine, lead azide, and lead styphanate, are extremely sensitive to friction, heat, and shock, making them dangerous to handle. They are mainly used in detonators or trigger devices attached to less sensitive secondary explosives—such as dynamite, TNT, HMX, PETN, or RDX (the base ingredient of many plastic explosives)—which require a smaller charge to set them off. Tertiary explosives—commonly called blasting agents—are the most stable of all, requiring a trigger charge of secondary explosives to cause detonation.

Ignition of explosive charges requires a series of events, variously known as the explosive train, the firing train, or the initiation sequence. For primary explosives, the "train" may be as simple as a sudden blow or vibration, such as accidentally dropping a bottle of nitroglycerine. Low-explosive charges are commonly set off by simple burning fuses—or, in firearms cartridges, by the firing of a primer charge, which lights the gunpowder.

High-explosive firing trains are more complicated, generally involving either two or three steps. A typical two-step sequence is the use of a detonator or blasting cap to set off dynamite. Other high explosives may require the three-step process, including a detonator to set off a booster charge of primary explosives, which then ignites the main charge.

While detonation of primary explosives requires only physical impact, their sensitivity limits usefulness and makes handling risky for all concerned. Secondary or tertiary explosives are required for any munitions or IED designed to be handled safely and fired from a launching device, or set to detonate at some specific future time or place (as at a chosen altitude above ground level or depth underwater).

The simplest detonation method, commonly used with black powder, dynamite, and fireworks, is a burning fuse that applies direct heat to the explosive charge. Various fuses burn at different speeds, and some burn underwater. The obvious weakness, for military or criminal applications, is a risk that the fuse may be discovered (by its sound, smell or smoke) and severed or extinguished prior to detonation.

Impact fuses, used in many kinds of military ordnance, operate on the same principle as the primers in firearms cartridges, detonating when the projectile strikes a solid object. Bombs and other projectiles with impact fuses may burrow into soft soil without exploding, and they constitute the largest class of UXOs and UXBs.

FBI VS. ATF

Responsibility for enforcing the Federal Explosives Control Statute is presently divided between the Federal Bureau of Investigation (FBI), created in 1908, and the younger Bureau of Alcohol, Tobacco, Firearms and Explosives (ATF), established as part of the U.S. Treasury Department in 1972. Officially, the FBI investigates terrorist bombings, while the ATF handles all other cases. The problem lies in defining "terrorism."

According to the FBI, "Domestic terrorism involves groups or individuals who are based and operate entirely within the United States and Puerto Rico without foreign direction and whose violent acts are directed at elements of the U.S. Government or population."[6] That said, however, the bureau has refused to investigate numerous cases that seem to fit its own broad definition.

The National Abortion Federation reports that since 1977, women's clinics nationwide have suffered at least 41 bombings, 96 attempted bombings or arsons, 175 arsons, 642 bomb threats, 1,404 acts of vandalism, and 100 "stink bomb" attacks carried out by the self-styled "Army of God" (AOG) and other antiabortion extremists. In 1993–94 "pro-life" gunmen killed four clinic employees and wounded two others. A doctor and his wife were also kidnapped, in violation of federal law. Still, despite that onslaught, FBI spokesmen declared in 1984 that its "Terrorism Section does not consider the 'Army of God' as a terrorist group, and therefore, no FBI investigation appears warranted at this time."[7]

Remote detonators may be triggered from a distance using wires or radio waves. Detonation is prevented if the wires are severed, and radio-remote detonation may be risky if the detonator is tuned to a common frequency, such as one used by two-way radios in taxis or emergency vehicles.

Proximity fuses detonate when the bomb or other device reaches a preset distance from its target. Such fuses may employ a number of devices to determine range, including radar, sonar, lasers, magnets,

FBI headquarters advised local victims and police to contact the ATF—which arrested the AOG's leaders and secured their conviction in federal court. ATF agents have also jailed various gangsters, neo-Nazis, Ku Klux Klansmen, "patriot militia" members, and others who carried out bombings. Ironically, the media has often credited FBI agents for those arrests.

Following the terrorist attacks of September 11, 2001, the ATF was transferred from Treasury to a new Department of Homeland Security, presumably cooperating with the FBI—but their rivalry continued. The chaotic result included a sting operation wherein FBI agents sold untaxed "bootleg" cigarettes to ATF officers, and clashes at various crime scenes where members of the hostile agencies threatened to arrest each other. Attorney General John Ashcroft tried to settle the dispute by giving ATF sole responsibility for training bomb-detection dogs and collecting statistics on bombings, but that concession solved nothing.

In May 2008 Michael Mason, former agent-in-charge of the FBI's Washington field office, told the *Washington Post,* "A lot of these things require a little adult supervision from the Justice Department or Congress, which will resolve a lot of the food fights these two agencies find themselves in." Officer Jeff Kirk, former commander of the Kokomo (Indiana) Police Department's bomb squad, said, "If you're working with one agency, you have to walk on eggshells if you mention the other. Frankly, after all these years, I'm really tired of this alphabet soup fight."

pressure gauges, passive acoustic monitors, and photoelectric cells, which may judge distance between a moving device and a stationary target, or vice versa.

Time delay fuses strive to detonate a bomb after a preselected period of time has passed. Such fuses may be chemical, electronic, mechanical, pyrotechnic, or some combination of two or more systems. Reliability of "time bombs" depends on a bomb-maker's skill, the quality of materials used, and any outside circumstances that may disable the timing device.

Sophisticated bombers often use one or more anti-handling devices to prevent deactivation of their explosive devices. The German *Luftwaffe* (Air Force) pioneered anti-handling mechanisms during its 1940 bombing campaign against England, and most nations use similar technology today. In military applications, anti-handling devices serve two functions: to kill bomb-disposal experts assigned to deactivate "duds," and to keep hostile forces from capturing ordnance for study.

Modern U.S. Army Field Manual No. 20-32, *Mine/Countermine Operations*, describes four basic types of anti-handling devices used on landmines, which may also apply to other ordnance and IEDs. They include the following:

- *Anti-lifting devices*, which detonate an explosive device when it is lifted or pulled from the place where it was found
- *Anti-disturbance devices*, also called "tilt/vibration switches," designed to detonate from any unexpected motion
- *Anti-defusing devices*, specifically designed to frustrate removal of the bomb's primary fuse
- *Anti-disarming devices*, which produce an explosion with any attempt to deactivate a bomb's arming mechanism[8]

Other forms of anti-handling devices include secondary pull fuses, concealed within a bomb and set to detonate if the primary fuse is extracted; anti-mine detector fuses, primed to detonate from exposure to the signals given off by standard electronic mine or metal detectors; and various electronic fuses sensitive to light, heat, or sound produced when a sealed bomb container is opened.

All such devices require special training and gear to protect bomb squad experts and let them deactivate explosives without injury to themselves, bystanders, or property.

Bombing

Natchez, Mississippi

Wharlest Jackson waited 12 years for a promotion at the Armstrong Rubber Company, where he started work in 1955. The holdup was not due to Jackson's skill, but rather to the color of his skin. As an African American in Mississippi, Jackson's life was ruled by segregation laws that limited his prospects. In addition, Armstrong's plant was a hotbed of racism, with members of the Ku Klux Klan (KKK) among its white employees.

To help himself and his family, Jackson joined the National Association for the Advancement of Colored People (NAACP), led in Natchez by fellow Armstrong worker George Metcalfe. Together, they campaigned for civil rights at Armstrong and throughout Adams County. In August 1965 a bomb in Metcalfe's car left him crippled for life. Jackson carried on the fight, and in February 1967 he won promotion to the "white" job of chemical mixer, receiving a pay raise of 17 cents per hour.

This was too much for the KKK to tolerate.

Jackson had learned to check his pickup truck for bombs each day before he left the factory. When he looked under its hood on February 27, he saw nothing—but he missed a time-bomb hidden underneath the driver's seat. He drove three blocks before the bomb exploded, killing him.

FBI agents blamed Jackson's murder—along with the Metcalfe bombing and other crimes—on the "Silver Dollar Group," a Klan faction

Police confer behind a roped-off area near a tarp-covered pickup truck and the truck's crumpled hood, which lies several feet away in the middle of a Natchez, Mississippi, street. Local Ku Klux Klan members planted a bomb in the truck of African-American civil rights leader Wharlest Jackson, who was fatally injured in the explosion. *(Bettmann/Corbis)*

whose members carried silver dollars minted in their birth years. Silver Dollar Klansmen were trained in the use of explosives and held weekend picnics where they practiced hiding bombs in cars. Despite that information, gathered from spies in the Klan, no one was charged with Jackson's murder in 1967, or when FBI agents reopened the case in 2005. It remains officially unsolved.

BOMBING FOR "FREEDOM"

As soldiers and engineers welcomed the development of explosives, so did political extremists. Among the first on record was Guy Fawkes (1570–1606), a British subject whose ancestors resisted separation of the Church of England from Catholicism in 1534, and were branded radical dissidents. Guy Fawkes spent 10 years fighting for the Catholic side in Europe's Wars of Religion, and was decorated for bravery in France in 1596.

Fawkes's training with explosives endeared him to a group of rebels led by Robert Catesby, who planned to assassinate King James I for his persecution of Catholics. Their plan, later named the Gunpowder Plot, was to detonate 1,800 pounds of gunpowder under Westminster Palace while James addressed members of Parliament and other Protestant officials on November 5, 1605.

One of the plotters changed his mind and warned authorities on October 26. Catesby learned of the leak, but decided to proceed when Fawkes checked the palace and found their 36 barrels of gunpowder undisturbed. Guy was preparing to light the fuse on November 5 when palace guards staged a last-minute search and surprised him. Under torture, he named Catesby and a dozen conspirators. A trial held on January 31, 1606, resulted in a sentence of death by disembowelment. Fawkes cheated his executioners by leaping from the gallows to break his own neck.

More than two centuries after the Gunpowder Plot, other rebels used explosives to dramatize their hatred of England. Members of the Irish Republican Brotherhood (IRB), organized in 1858, tried various protest tactics before they turned to bombing in January 1881. Targets included a police station and other government buildings in Liverpool; a police barracks in Edinburgh, Scotland; the Lord Mayor's home and the *Times* newspaper office in London; plus a gasworks and railway depot in Glasgow, Scotland. In October 1882 police arrested Thomas Gallagher and five other IRB members, seizing 400 pounds of explosives earmarked for use against Parliament.

The IRB's bombing campaign prompted creation of a new London police unit, the Special Irish Branch (SIB), in March 1883. While not a bomb squad in the modern sense, the SIB focused on counterterrorism work. Later, its leaders dropped the "Irish" tag, continuing as the Special Branch, with expanded duties including protection of British VIPs and security patrols at airports and seaports.

While IRB bombings waned in the mid-1880s, the group survived and played a leading role in Ireland's War of Independence (1919–21), which created the Irish Republic. After the establishment of the Irish Republic, England still controlled six counties in Ulster, known since

1921 as Northern Ireland. That lingering British presence, aggravated by the Ulster Protestant majority's persecution of Catholics, sparked more violence by the Irish Republican Army (IRA), established in 1913. The IRA detonated more than 50 bombs in England during 1939–40, then confined its activities to Northern Ireland over the next two decades.[1]

Widespread Irish violence resumed with the formation of a Protestant terrorist group, the loyalist Ulster Volunteer Force, in May 1966. Both sides in the ensuing 40-year conflict used bombs and other weapons to terrorize their opponents. The Official IRA renounced terrorism in August 1969, prompting formation of a new Provisional Irish Republican Army (PIRA), which expanded operations from Northern Ireland to England and beyond. Before a final cease-fire was achieved in 2006, the struggle produced at least 2,392 violent deaths and 47,541 injuries to civilians, 16,209 bombings and attempted bombings, 36,923 shootings, 2,225 arsons, and 19,605 arrests for terrorist activity.[2]

Finding skillful bombers posed a problem for the PIRA. One bomb-maker built IEDs with safety pins, which had to be removed before the timing fuse would activate. Some PIRA members were afraid to pull the pin and left their bombs as useless duds. The bomb-maker then added tags with his address, requiring those who planted the bombs to return both pin and tag or face painful punishment. Inevitably, one forgot his orders, and the address tag led police to the bomb-maker's doorstep.[3]

In response to the Irish "Troubles," as they were called, London's Metropolitan Police Service created a new Anti-Terrorist Branch in the early 1970s, in collaboration with the Special Branch. In 2005 administrators merged the Special Branch and Anti-Terrorist Branch to create a new Counter Terrorism Command, whose more than 1,500 members include London's bomb-disposal squad and specialists in dealing with chemical, biological, radiological, and nuclear weapons.

Since World War II the Middle East has spawned more violence than Northern Ireland, with impact felt around the globe. And while modern media portrayals of Middle Eastern mayhem focus chiefly on Muslim extremists, the terrorism actually began with agents of the Irgun and Lehi, militant Zionist groups dedicated to driving British authorities out of Palestine and creating a Jewish homeland. Between

April 1938 and May 1948 Irgun/Lehi terrorists detonated more than 60 bombs throughout Palestine, killing at least 509 victims and injuring at least 664. The same terrorists also sent letter bombs to British leaders and bombed targets in London, Rome, Germany, Cyprus, and Lebanon. Irgun and Lehi assassins also killed at least 150 victims in sniping attacks.[4]

While Zionist spokesmen described those crimes as "self-defense" against violent Arabs, future Israeli prime minister David Ben Gurion (1886–1973) said, "Let us not ignore the truth among ourselves. . . . Politically we are the aggressors and they [Arabs] defend themselves."[5] Irgun commander Menachem Begin (1913–92) served as Israel's prime minister during 1977–83. Former Lehi leader Yitzhak Shamir served as prime minister in 1983–84 and again in 1986–92.

British authorities in Palestine relied on experts from the Royal Army Ordnance Corps (RAOC) Ammunition Examiners to disarm terrorist bombs between 1945 and 1948, when international agreements created the state of Israel. The RAOC was organized in 1875, with duties limited primarily to storage of army munitions until World War I, when the Ammunition Examiners unit was formed to deal with new time-delay fuses on German artillery shells. Their work continued with UXBs in World War II, and left the group well suited to disarm IEDs in British-occupied regions after the war.

Sadly, the creation of Israel only increased Middle Eastern violence, as Muslim neighbors waged violent campaigns against the new state and its allies worldwide. No comprehensive tally of bombings spawned by hatred of Israel exists, but the following cases stand out among thousands:

- *October 23, 1983:* Suicide bombers destroyed a U.S. Marine Corps barracks in Beirut, Lebanon, killing 242 American servicemen.
- *December 21, 1988:* Terrorists bombed Pan American Airlines Flight 103 over Lockerbie, Scotland, killing all 259 people aboard.
- *August 7, 1998:* Bombs detonated by al-Qaeda terrorists at U.S. embassies in Kenya and Tanzania killed a total of 301 victims and wounded at least 5,095.
- *December 2–3, 2001:* Suicide bombers in Israel killed 25 people and wounded nearly 200 in two explosions in Haifa and Jerusalem.[6]

Long before Israel's enemies struck on American soil, Puerto Rican nationalists fought to end U.S. control of their homeland. Rebel gunmen tried to assassinate President Harry Truman in 1950 and shot

"DYNAMITE BOB"

Few terrorists worldwide—and fewer still in the United States—have enjoyed longer criminal careers than Robert Edward Chambliss (1904–85). Born in Alabama, where laws enforced white supremacy, Chambliss grew up a bitter racist and joined the Ku Klux Klan in 1924. Although suspected of various crimes, Chambliss did not become notorious until the late 1940s, when African Americans filed lawsuits to open Birmingham's "white" neighborhoods to people of all races.

During 1947–51 racist bombings were so common in Birmingham that some locals dubbed it "Bombingham," while the city's black ghetto was nicknamed "Dynamite Hill."

After a period of calm in Birmingham, bombings resumed with the Supreme Court's ruling on school integration. The terrorism resumed in January 1962, with three bombings in one night, and continued through 1963.

So far, Chambliss had killed no one, but that changed on September 15, 1963, when he bombed the Sixteenth Street Baptist Church. Four girls died in that blast, forcing police and FBI agents to conduct a serious investigation. Alabama Governor George Wallace—elected in 1962 on a promise of "segregation forever"—ordered state police to charge Chambliss and two other suspects with misdemeanor counts of illegal dynamite possession. They paid small fines and FBI agents dropped the case, fearing embarrassment if white jurors acquitted Chambliss of murder.

Justice was slow in overtaking Dynamite Bob. Fourteen years passed before Alabama Attorney General William Baxley indicted Chambliss for murder. Jurors convicted him in 1977, resulting in a life prison term. Chambliss died in custody on October 29, 1985.

up Congress four years later, but those raids achieved nothing. Later, between 1974 and 1983, the Armed Forces of National Liberation (FALN) detonated more than 120 bombs throughout the United States, killing six people and wounding more than 70 others. Advance warnings let police deactivate some of the IEDs, and numerous FALN members were imprisoned. Their arrests prompted another 22 bombings by an allied group, the Organization of Volunteers for the Puerto Rican Revolution, between 1986 and 1990.[7]

WHITE TERROR

Not all of America's terrorists are revolutionaries. Others, like the KKK, use explosives to stall the march of progress toward equality for citizens of every race, religion, and ethnic background.

After the Civil War, the original Klan killed thousands of victims during Reconstruction (1865–77), while burning homes, schools, churches—and one whole Arkansas town—but its members steered clear of explosives. When the KKK revived in 1915, it railed against new enemies and used new weapons. Dynamite proved popular, highlighted by two cases from 1926, when Canadian Klansmen bombed a Catholic church and a Michigan KKK leader killed three people with a parcel bomb mailed to a political opponent. Several Klan chapters even bombed their own headquarters, seeking public sympathy.[8]

Klan violence waned during the Great Depression, then resumed after World War II, with the growth of the African-American civil rights movement. Between 1947 and 1953 authorities recorded 36 bombings by the KKK and allied groups, one-third of them occurring in Birmingham, Alabama. Florida and Tennessee also suffered bombing campaigns, including a blast that killed Florida NAACP leader Harry Moore and his wife in 1951. Those crimes remain officially unsolved.[9]

The U.S. Supreme Court's 1954 ban on school segregation sparked a new rash of terrorism, with media sources reporting 195 racist bombings and arson attacks by year's end. Researcher Barbara Patterson counted another 148 Klan-type bombings between January 1956 and May 1963. Mississippi's White Knights of the KKK bombed or burned at least 158 buildings, five vehicles, and a baseball park between 1963 and 1968. More Klan bombings rocked Houston, Texas, and Pontiac,

Michigan, in 1970–71, striking radio stations, political offices, and school buses.[10]

Despite the high number of racist bombings, only seven lives were lost between 1951 and 1967, including the Moores, Wharlest Jackson, and four girls killed in a Birmingham, Alabama, church. However, America's most deadly bombing—the Oklahoma City blast that killed 168 in 1995—was carried out by one-time Klansman Timothy McVeigh.

The formation of a (short-lived) Southern Conference on Bombing in 1958 had little effect: White police in the South rarely investigated Klan bombings, and sometimes accused the victims of bombing themselves. Some lawmen, such as Birmingham Police Commissioner Eugene "Bull" Connor (1897–1973), actively supported the KKK and made personal bomb threats to civil rights activists.[11]

MAD BOMBERS

According to the FBI, mentally unstable *serial bombers* strike as a result of motives that include revenge, personal excitement, and extreme religious beliefs.[12] Hungarian bomber Sylvestre Matuschka, a former officer of the Austro-Hungarian Army, enjoyed watching train wrecks, which he caused by dynamiting railroad tracks. Before his 1931 arrest he killed 22 people and injured 120.[13] More recent examples of serial bombers include the following:

- *Theodore Kaczynski*, a math professor who left teaching in 1971, at age 27, to live as a hermit, mailed or planted 16 bombs between 1978 and 1995, targeting airlines and universities—which earned him his "Unabomber" nickname. Police defused two of Kaczynski's bombs, but the rest killed three victims and injured 21.[14] Captured in 1996, he received a life prison term.
- *Eric Rudolph*, a religious fanatic who detonated four bombs in Georgia and Alabama during 1996–98, killed two people and

---

(opposite page) Former University of California—Berkeley math professor Theodore John Kaczynski is escorted into the federal courthouse in Helena, Montana, in April 1996. Kaczynski was later sentenced to life in prison for the 16 bombs he planted, which killed three people and injured 21. *(Associated Press)*

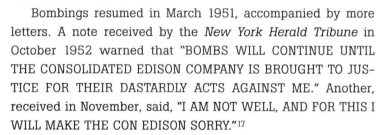

GEORGE METESKY (1903–94)

America's first serial bomber plagued New York City between 1940 and 1956, planting 33 bombs which injured 15 persons.[15] Targets included public transportation terminals, theaters, libraries, and office buildings.

The "Mad Bomber's" first IED, found at a Consolidated Edison power plant in November 1940, came with a note signed "F.P.," reading: "CON EDISON CROOKS—THIS IS FOR YOU." The second, left five blocks from Con Ed headquarters in September 1941, was followed by a letter promising no more bombs during World War II, but warning that "LATER I WILL BRING THE CON EDISON TO JUSTICE—THEY WILL PAY FOR THEIR DASTARDLY DEEDS."[16]

Bombings resumed in March 1951, accompanied by more letters. A note received by the *New York Herald Tribune* in October 1952 warned that "BOMBS WILL CONTINUE UNTIL THE CONSOLIDATED EDISON COMPANY IS BROUGHT TO JUSTICE FOR THEIR DASTARDLY ACTS AGAINST ME." Another, received in November, said, "I AM NOT WELL, AND FOR THIS I WILL MAKE THE CON EDISON SORRY."[17]

wounded at least 150 more.[18] Targets included two women's clinics, a gay bar, and Atlanta's Centennial Olympic Park. Arrested in 2003, Rudolph received five consecutive life terms.

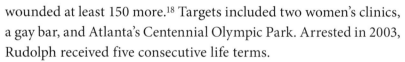

- *David Copeland*, a British neo-Nazi, carried out a two-week bombing campaign against London's black, Asian, and gay residents during April 1999. Each bomb contained 1,500 nails; their blasts caused three deaths and 129 injuries.[19] Convicted of murder in June 2000, he received six life sentences.

OPPOSING TERROR

Neither Britain's Special Branch nor America's first "bomb squad," formed in 1903, were trained to disarm IEDs. Rather, they focused on identifying bombers and infiltrating radical groups to prevent attacks. Dedicated

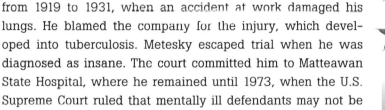

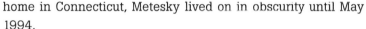

In 1956 police consulted forensic psychiatrist James Brussel, whose profile labeled the bomber an unmarried, middle-aged man, living with a female relative in Connecticut. When arrested, Brussel predicted, he would be wearing a double-breasted suit with the jacket buttoned. Publication of that profile in December brought three more letters from the bomber and led police to the Connecticut home where 53-year-old George Metesky lived with two of his sisters. While captured in pajamas, Metesky dressed for jail in a double-breasted suit with the jacket buttoned.

Detectives learned that Metesky had worked for Con Ed from 1919 to 1931, when an accident at work damaged his lungs. He blamed the company for the injury, which developed into tuberculosis. Metesky escaped trial when he was diagnosed as insane. The court committed him to Matteawan State Hospital, where he remained until 1973, when the U.S. Supreme Court ruled that mentally ill defendants may not be held in prison hospitals without trial. Released to his family home in Connecticut, Metesky lived on in obscurity until May 1994.

bomb-disposal teams emerged after World War I in response to a rash of political attacks. The bombing of the San Francisco Preparedness Day parade (which was held to celebrate the inevitable entry of the United States to war) killed 10 and wounded 40 in July 1916, and a blast on New York's Wall Street killed 38 and injured 400 in September 1920.[20]

Those crimes, and the availability of military veterans trained in UXO disposal, marked the beginning of true U.S. bomb squads. The modern spread of terrorism, accompanied by more sophisticated IEDs and weapons of mass destruction such as biological, chemical, and nuclear weapons, has demanded more intensive bomb-squad training and development of new equipment to prevent disasters.

Following the 9/11 terrorist attacks, the U.S. Department of Homeland Security (DHS) was created to coordinate various national security measures, including a new Office of Bombing Prevention (OBP). According to its mission statement,

> The Office for Bombing Prevention develops tools to improve national preparedness for bombing threats at all levels of government, the public, and within the private sector . . . coordinates the Department's Combating Terrorist Use of Explosives programs to deter, detect, prevent, protect against, and respond to IED (Improvised Explosive Device) threats . . . [and] coordinates IED programs across the Department, including collaborating with the Science and Technology Directorate to identify and manage counter-IED research and development.[21]

In practical terms, the OBP "provides a uniform analysis of bomb squad, explosives detection canine team, dive team, and other key bombing prevention components' capabilities," and sponsors the Technical Resource for Incident Prevention (TRIPwire), described as "a secure, online, collaborative information-sharing network for bomb squads, law enforcement, and other emergency services personnel to learn more about current terrorist improvised explosive device (IED) tactics, techniques, and procedures, including design and emplacement considerations."[22]

Underworld Bombing

Phoenix, Arizona

Reporter Don Bolles was known for embarrassing Arizona's rich and powerful citizens. In 1974 he exposed corrupt businessman Kemper Marley's large donations to governor-elect Raul Castro, and two years later his articles blocked Castro's appointment of Marley to Arizona's Racing Commission, a post where Marley's underworld connections dating from the 1920s could have made him richer, still. At the same time, Bolles tackled Emprise Corporation—a nationwide sports concession firm with links to organized crime—and turned a spotlight on its business inside the Grand Canyon state.

Somewhere along the line, Bolles made enemies who hated him enough to kill him.

Around 1:30 P.M. on June 2, 1976, Bolles left a Phoenix restaurant where he had scheduled a meeting with one of his sources. The man didn't show, and Bolles got into his car to leave. Seconds later, a powerful bomb wrecked the vehicle, pitching him into the street. As help arrived, Bolles gasped, "They finally got me. . . the Mafia. . . Emprise. . . Find John."[1] Bolles died from his injuries on June 13.

Police identified "John" as John Harvey Adamson, the source who kept Bolles waiting on June 2. Adamson admitted building the bomb and placing it in Bolles's car, and named two accomplices. Kemper Marley associate Max Dunlap allegedly hired Adamson for the job, while plumber James Robison triggered the blast by remote control. Adamson received a life sentence for second-degree murder in 1977, and then testified against Dunlap and Robison, both of whom were sentenced to die in January 1978. No charges were filed against Marley, who died in 1990, at age 83.

Arizona's Supreme Court overturned the Dunlap-Robison verdicts in 1980, and Adamson refused to testify at their new trials, thus violating his 1977 plea-bargain. Authorities dismissed the charges against Dunlap and Robison, then convicted Adamson of first-degree murder and sentenced him to death. A federal court reversed that verdict in 1986. State authorities filed new charges against Dunlap and Robison in 1990. Jurors convicted Dunlap again in 1993, resulting in a life sentence, but Robison won acquittal at a second trial; he then confessed plotting Adamson's murder and received a five-year sentence for that crime. Adamson entered the federal Witness Security Program in 1996.[2]

City and federal investigators examine a car damaged in June 1976 in Phoenix, Arizona, in a bomb explosion that fatally injured investigative reporter Don Bolles. *(Associated Press)*

MEET THE MOB

Federal law defines organized crime (or racketeering) as "the unlawful activities of . . . a highly organized, disciplined association" committed for profit. Various acts associated with organized crime include murder, kidnapping, arson, robbery, illegal gambling, dealing in controlled substances or other contraband, extortion, bribery, fraud, embezzlement, human trafficking, money laundering, and terrorism.[3] While some such groups—like the Mafia, Chinese Triads, and Japanese Yakuza—limit membership to a specific nationality, organized crime transcends racial and religious lines.

America's first taste of what the FBI calls traditional organized crime came from "Black Hand" extortionists, Italians who terrorized their fellow immigrants from the 1880s through the early 1920s. Most were criminals before they came to the United States, and they persisted in that vein, threatening Italian-American merchants with bombings or death if they failed to pay for "protection." The written threats were signed with handprints in black ink, thus explaining their nickname. Recalling police corruption at home, most victims paid up and refused to testify against their tormentors until the New York Police Department (NYPD) organized a special "bomb squad" under Lieutenant Giuseppe Petrosino to pursue the criminals.[4]

While some Black Handers were jailed or deported, most quit the business when Prohibition (1920–33) made them rich from peddling bootleg beer and whiskey. Their bombing skills proved useful in the "dry" years, during gang wars and attempts to dominate American labor unions. Cornelius Shea (1872–1929), founding president of the International Brotherhood of Teamsters from 1903–07, faced multiple charges arising from his work with Chicago gangsters, but he served only one short prison term for attempted murder. In May 1921 police blamed him for a series of bombings related to a local strike, but they lacked sufficient evidence to file charges.[5]

Mobster Al Capone spared no effort to crush his Chicago rivals during the Roaring Twenties, including ruthless control of local politics. During the spring primary elections of 1928, Capone gangsters threw 61 bombs at various targets, leading reporters to call it the "Pineapple Primary" (after the shape of hand grenades). Two leaders of the rival Republican party were also shot dead for opposing Capone's Democrats.[6]

Thirty years later, Youngstown, Ohio, suffered so many underworld bombings that locals began to call it "Bomb City, USA," while the phrase "Youngstown tuneup" referred to car-bombing.[7] The most notorious case involved Mafia gangster Charles "Cadillac Charlie" Cavallaro, who died with his 11-year-old son in a November 1962 car-bombing. A second child survived the blast.

Cleveland, 60 miles west of Youngstown, endured its own nine-year bombing campaign, as syndicate leaders tried to dispose of rogue gangster Danny "The Irishman" Greene. The trouble began in May 1968, when longtime mobster Alex "Shondor" Birns (1907–75) hired Greene to bomb an African-American gambler's office. Greene botched the job, destroying his own car and leaving himself permanently deaf in one ear, then determined to use professional bomb-makers in the future. In September 1970 Greene hired Art Sneperger to kill union leader "Big Mike" Frato with a car bomb, but Sneperger—a part-time police informer—betrayed the plan to authorities. Curiously, Sneperger died when another bomb exploded in Frato's car a year later, perhaps as a result of radio interference with his remote-control detonator.

Gunmen finally killed Frato in December 1971, prompting Mafia retaliation against Greene. Snipers sent by Shondor Birns missed Greene, as did the bombers who wired a charge to his car's ignition. Greene struck back with a car bomb that killed Birns outside a Cleveland church in March 1975. Two months later, another bomb demolished Greene's apartment, but he and a girlfriend escaped unharmed. Greene's next bomb was meant for mobster Alfred Calabrese, but it killed a neighbor who tried to move Calabrese's double-parked car. Thirty-seven bombs rocked Cleveland during 1977, earning it the title "Bombing Capital of America," but Greene could not defeat the large syndicate. A remote-control car bomb killed him outside of his dentist's office in October 1977, finally ending the war.[8]

THE "HONORED SOCIETY"

Sicily's traditional Mafia—ironically known as the "Honored Society"[9]—turned from "normal" gangland murders to terrorist tactics in

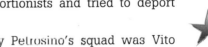

GIUSEPPE PETROSINO (1860–1909)

Italian native "Joe" Petrosino came to the United States with his parents at age 14 and joined the NYPD in October 1883. His arrival and advancement to detective sergeant in 1895 coincided with the rise of Black Hand terrorism in New York City's Little Italy district. In 1903, promoted again to lieutenant, Petrosino was assigned to lead the department's "bomb squad," also known as the Italian Squad for its focus on immigrant felons. The team was not trained to disarm IEDs, but rather arrested Black Hand extortionists and tried to deport them as undesirable aliens.

One gangster sent home by Petrosino's squad was Vito Cascio Ferro, a leader of the local Mafia until his deportation. Ferro never forgave Petrosino, and he was waiting in 1909 when Petrosino visited Sicily to examine police records. On March 12, while waiting to meet an informant in downtown Palermo, Petrosino was killed by unknown gunmen. Police detained Ferro but could never prove his guilt. He was jailed for another slaying in 1927 and died in prison 16 years later.

The NYPD's bomb squad was disbanded in 1911 and then revived in 1914 to investigate "Bolshevik radicals." Its members still lacked any IED-disposal training, and their violent interrogation methods earned them what authors Richard Esposito and Ted Gerstein call "an unsavory reputation as a group of thugs."[10] A more professional approach prevailed from 1926 onward, including special classes in code-breaking and bomb-disposal techniques proved effective by the U.S. military.

the late 20th century, declaring open war against prosecutors, police, and informers who tried to break the organization's monopoly on local organized crime. The first prominent victims, prosecutor Cesare Terranova and General Carlo Chiesa, were shot in 1979 and 1982, respectively, but the Mafia soon turned to bombing as a more dramatic means of murder.

Victim Rocco Chinnici (1925–83) began serving as a judge in 1952, and then switched to prosecuting gangsters in 1966. By 1979 he was Palermo's chief prosecutor, replacing Cesare Terranova. He created a special unit on organized crime, the Antimafia Pool, which included courageous magistrates Giovanni Falcone and Paolo Borsellino. Chinnici was next to feel the Mafia's wrath; on July 29, 1983, a car bomb exploded outside his apartment building, killing Chinnici, two of his bodyguards, and the building's caretaker.

Police learned that the bomb was triggered by Giuseppe "Pino" Greco, one of the Mafia's most prolific killers, on orders from his uncle, "godfather" Michele Greco, whom Giovanni Falcone had indicted with 14 others on July 9 for the 1982 assassination of Carlo Chiesa. Michele Greco was captured in 1986, facing trial on charges of ordering 78 murders. Convicted in 1987, he received a life sentence and died in prison on February 13, 2008. His nephew remained at large, but was convicted *in absentia* of 58 murders; some investigators blamed him for 80 to 300 slayings. Pino Greco eluded police, but Mafia gunmen killed him in September 1985.[11]

Giovanni Falcone (1939–92) was next on the Mafia's hit list. Bombers caught up with him on May 23, 1992, outside Capaci, as he was being escorted to Palermo's airport. A 770-pound explosive charge buried under the highway demolished Falcone's car, killing him along with his wife and three of his bodyguards. Eight weeks later, on July 19, a car bomb killed Paolo Borsellino and five policemen in Palermo. Both bombings were ordered by Mafia boss Salvatore "The Beast" Riina, a fugitive who was captured in January 1993. Hitman Giovanni Brusca confessed to the Falcone bombing and turned state's evidence against Riina. After much delay, Riina and 18 other gangsters were convicted of the murders and sentenced to prison in November 2000. Still, the Mafia remains strong in Italy, banking an estimated $133 billion per year (15 percent of the nation's gross national product).[12]

NARCOTERRORISM

A similar situation exists in South America, where huge profits from cocaine have corrupted many government officials, placing honest prosecutors and police at constant risk of death. Peruvian President Fernando Belaúnde Terry (1912–2002) coined the term *narcoterrorism* in 1983, describing attacks on public officials by criminal groups such as Colombia's Medellín drug cartel.

Colombian drug lords sometimes collaborate with paramilitary groups in acts of terrorism, as in the November 1985 attack on Bogotá's Palace of Justice by guerrillas of the "M-19" movement, which killed 85 hostages, including 11 of Colombia's 25 Supreme Court justices who had threatened to prosecute drug cartel leaders.[13]

The Medellín Cartel declared "total and absolute war" against the Colombian government in 1989, launching a wave of terrorism that included the following incidents:

- *May 30, 1989*: A Bogotá car-bombing kills four victims and wounds 37; the bomb misses the country's top security officer.
- *September 2, 1989*: A car-bombing of Bogotá's leading newspaper leaves 84 injured.
- *October 16, 1989*: Another newspaper office is bombed in Bucaramanga, killing four persons.
- *November 27, 1989*: A cartel bomb destroys Avianca Flight 203 over Bogotá, killing 110. The presumed target, presidential candidate César Gaviria Trujillo, missed the flight.
- *December 6, 1989*: A 1,100-pound bomb explodes outside the Bogotá headquarters of Colombia's Administrative Department of Security, killing 50, wounding more than 600, and destroying more than 300 surrounding shops.
- *May 13, 1990*: Two bombs explode at Bogotá shopping malls, killing 14 and wounding more than 100.
- *February 16, 1991*: A 400-pound car bomb kills 22 people at a bull-ring in Medellín.
- *July 16, 1992*: Two cartel car bombs kill 24 victims in Lima, Peru.
- *January 30, 1993*: Another Bogotá car bomb kills 20 victims.
- *April 15, 1993*: A car bomb kills 15 and wounds more than 100 at a Bogotá shopping mall.
- *December 8, 2002*: A car bomb wounds 50 people in a Bogotá suburb.
- *February 7, 2003*: Yet another Bogotá car bomb claims 36 lives.
- *October 7, 2003*: A car bomb explodes outside a Bogotá nightclub, killing two policemen and four civilians.[14]

In May 2005, in response to those crimes, the ATF conducted an explosives training course in Bogotá for 30 agents of the Colombian Attorney General's Office, National Police, federal police, and coroner's office. The course included "improvised explosive devices, post-blast scene investigation, forensic lab reconstruction, bomber motivation and investigative leads, a practical exercise at an ordnance range, bomb threat management, and country case studies." Prior to those classes, in 2004 ATF experts had also trained Colombia's first team of arson investigators.[15]

TUCSON MAFIA BOMBINGS (1968–69)

Starting in the 1930s, various Eastern and Midwestern gangsters purchased homes and businesses in Arizona, where they found the climate pleasant and the political corruption profitable. The most prominent Mafia members to settle in Tucson were Detroit's Peter Licavoli and New York's Joseph Bonanno. Despite competing interests, they lived in peace until July 1968, when a series of bombings sparked fears of a nationwide gang war.

The first bomb exploded at Bonanno's home on July 26, followed over the next 12 months by blasts at Licavoli's ranch, the homes of other mobsters, and various shops owned by members of organized crime. In September 1968 Arizona congressman Morris Udahl (1922–98) asked FBI Director J. Edgar Hoover (1895–1972) to increase the number of agents in Arizona in order to prevent Udahl's state from becoming "the future criminal playground of America." Hoover complied, noting the "increasing number of racket figures" in Tucson.[16]

In fact, however, mobsters weren't the problem. They were only the targets.

In the summer of 1969 a local thug named Jerry Pasley approached Tucson police and admitted planting the bombs with a friend, Walter Prideaux. They were paid to set the bombs, Pasley claimed, by Tucson FBI Agent David Olin Hale. "I didn't know what was going on," Pasley said. "I was a little bit confused and in the dark, too. I mean, I knew he was an FBI guy. But I didn't know if he was a renegade or working for

THE HOME FRONT

The ATF has pursued members of organized crime since the agency's creation in 1972, filing charges related to untaxed liquor and tobacco, illegal firearms, and explosives. Some of its successes in that endless war on crime include the following:

- *July 1976*: Agents in Orlando, Florida, arrest Paul Parker—president of Teamster Union Local 385—and 11 others for multiple bombings. All are convicted, receiving 100-year prison terms.

J. Edgar Hoover or the CIA or what. He had us all pretty much confused down there."[17]

The news stunned Arizona and sent shockwaves all the way to Washington, D.C., where FBI headquarters scrambled to minimize embarrassment. Hale left the bureau without punitive action, while the FBI moved swiftly to close the investigation. Hoover aide Mark Felt—later identified as the Watergate scandal's "Deep Throat" informant—wrote: "While Hale [was] not fully forthright in [his] interview and amended his answers several times, he is extremely emphatic in denial of guilt in bombings and in his belief that it is [a Mafia] plot to discredit him and the Bureau."[18]

In fact, however, the FBI had tried to start at least one other Mafia gang war in America less than two years before the first Tucson bombing. Files released under the Freedom of Information Act document "Operation Hoodwink," a plot by agents in New York to provoke violence between the Mafia and the U.S. Communist Party (CPUSA) by printing forged leaflets in which the party appeared to denounce sweatshops run by the mob. The stated goal was "to provoke a bitter dispute between the two organizations." Hoover approved the plan on October 5, 1966, adding a personal suggestion that "thought should also be given to initiating spurious [Mafia] attacks on the CPUSA, so that each group would think the other was mounting a campaign against it." The plot later expanded to Philadelphia, but never produced the violence that Hoover desired.[19]

- *April 1978*: The car-bomb murder of mobster Salvatore Gingello in Rochester, New York, prompts an investigation capped in January 1980 by the conviction of seven Mafia members sentenced to 137 years in prison.
- *November 1978*: An ATF investigation of bombings and arsons around Tacoma, Washington, produces the arrest of mobster John Carbone, his son, and five others. Six defendants plead guilty, while Sheriff George Janovich Sr. is convicted at trial on bribery charges.
- *July 2003*: Agents in Arizona raid 18 homes and clubhouses occupied by members of the Hells Angels motorcycle gang, arresting 36 suspects on charges of bomb-making, murder for hire, and drug violations.[20]
- *December 2006*: ATF agents lead raids to arrest eight members of New York City's Gambino and Genovese Mafia "families." Charges filed against the eight include bombing, arson, murder, extortion, obstruction of justice, loan sharking, and racketeering conspiracy.

Mail Bombs

Atlanta, Georgia

Thomas William Hardwick (1872–1944) was a hard-line conservative whose views and actions sometimes provoked violent sentiments. As a Georgia state legislator from 1898 to 1902, he joined the movement to strip African Americans of their right to vote while imposing rigid "Jim Crow" segregation of the races. Later, as a member of the U.S. Senate, he sponsored the Anarchist Exclusion Act, banning immigrants who opposed organized government from the United States after October 1918.

On April 29, 1919, a package arrived at Hardwick's Georgia home. It was wrapped in green paper and had a stamp that read "Gimbel Brothers Novelty Samples." Hardwick's housekeeper opened the package, triggering a bomb concealed inside. The blast tore off her hands, while Hardwick's wife suffered burns to her face and neck, with several teeth broken by shrapnel.

The day before Hardwick's bombing, an identical package arrived at the office of Seattle Mayor Ole Hanson, who had recently crushed an anarchist strike in his city. An aide, William Langer, opened the wrong end of the parcel, whereupon a vial of acid meant to detonate the blasting cap fell out and shattered on his desk. Langer gave the bomb to police, who notified the U.S. Post Office.

On April 30 a postal inspector in New York City recognized 16 more of the "Gimbel Brothers" bombs. Twelve more were intercepted en route to their intended targets, which included the U.S. Attorney General; Secretary of Labor and Postmaster General; Supreme Court Justice Oliver Wendell Holmes; five other members of Congress; the governors of Mississippi and Pennsylvania; New York City's mayor and police commissioner; various state and city officials; and two mil-

WALTER LEROY MOODY

On December 16, 1989, a parcel bomb filled with nails exploded at the Birmingham, Alabama, home of Robert Vance, a judge of the Eleventh Circuit Court of Appeals, which reviews federal cases from Alabama, Florida, and Georgia. Two days later, a similar bomb detonated in the office of Robert Robinson, a lawyer in Savannah, Georgia. Two more bombs were received at Savannah's federal courthouse (which houses the Eleventh Circuit Court of Appeals) and at an NAACP office in Jacksonville, Florida.

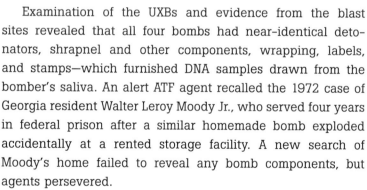

Examination of the UXBs and evidence from the blast sites revealed that all four bombs had near-identical detonators, shrapnel and other components, wrapping, labels, and stamps—which furnished DNA samples drawn from the bomber's saliva. An alert ATF agent recalled the 1972 case of Georgia resident Walter Leroy Moody Jr., who served four years in federal prison after a similar homemade bomb exploded accidentally at a rented storage facility. A new search of Moody's home failed to reveal any bomb components, but agents persevered.

In April 1990 an informant told ATF agents that shortly before the bombings, he had sold Moody black powder and primers identical to those used in the parcel bombs. In June 1991 a federal jury convicted Moody on 71 felony counts, prompting imposition of a life prison term. Alabama authorities later tried him for Judge Vance's murder, and Moody received a death sentence for that crime in 1997. He remains in prison today, still appealing both verdicts, while conspiracy theories muddy the waters surrounding his case.

lionaire industrialists, J.P. Morgan and John Rockefeller.[1] Authorities blamed the April bombs—and others detonated during June 1919—on followers of anarchist Luigi Galleani (1861–1931), but while hundreds of "enemy aliens" were jailed and deported during 1919–20, the bombers were never identified.

OPEN WITH CARE

Mail bombs, also commonly described as *letter, post,* or *parcel bombs,* rank among the oldest and most persistent weapons in the arsenal of terrorism. They are normally designed to detonate when opened, thereby injuring or killing the recipient. As in the Hardwick case, however, mail is often opened by someone other than the addressee—a fact that terrorists are bound to recognize.

The first known mail bomb was described in the diary of Danish historian Bolle Luxdorph (1716–88). An entry dated January 18, 1764, describes an explosive package sent to the home of a Colonel Poulsen, in the town of Børglum, who was "very injured" but survived. A month later, Poulsen received a letter written in German, promising a larger bomb to come, but the threat was not carried out and the bomber was never identified. Another reference in Luxdorph's diary reports a second mail bombing by persons unknown in 1764, in the Italian province of Savona.[2]

The next reported mail bombing occurred 125 years later, in 1889. Edward White, a 61-year-old employee of Madame Tussauds wax museum in London, lost his job in February and retaliated by sending a bomb to the museum. Grains of gunpowder leaked from the package and betrayed its contents, landing White in jail.[3]

Seven years after the bungled anarchist bombings, in 1926, a Michigan Ku Klux Klan leader ran for public office in Muskegon, Michigan, and lost. Enraged, he sent a mail bomb to the home of his victorious opponent, killing three people and earning himself a life sentence in prison. Twelve years later, a parcel bomb mailed from Chihuahua City killed the mayor of Juarez, Mexico.[4]

The Zionist campaign against Arabs and British forces in Palestine included the world's first international mail-bombings during 1947–48. In June 1947 officers of London's Scotland Yard intercepted 20 letter bombs, mailed from Italy by Lehi terrorists, addressed to British officials including Foreign Secretary Ernest Bevin (1881–1951) and future prime minister Anthony Eden (1897–1977). In September 1947 a bomb addressed to the British War Office exploded in a London post office, injuring two people. On May 3, 1938, a Sternist letter bomb addressed to a Royal Army officer in Colverhampton, England, killed the officer's brother. Eight days later another Zionist parcel bomb was defused at the home of General Evelyn Barker (1894–1983), former commander of British troops in Palestine.[5]

Zionists did not abandon mail bombs when the state of Israel was created in 1948. Such weapons also proved useful against Nazi war criminals, such as Alois Brunner, commander of a concentration camp in France where an estimated 140,000 Jews died between June 1943 and August 1944. Although sentenced to death by a French court *in absentia*, Brunner was never captured. His fate remains unknown, but Israeli agents wounded him twice with letter bombs, in 1961 and 1980.[6]

In January 1968 a group of Cuban exiles living in America launched a mail-bombing campaign against the government of Prime Minister Fidel Castro. The first bomb, mailed from New York City, wounded five workers at a Havana post office on January 9. Sixteen days later, two more bombs exploded in Miami before they could be mailed to Cuba. Thereafter, the group—El Poder Cubano ("Cuban Power")—satisfied itself with bombs planted by hand. During 1974 other exile groups sent bombs to Cuban diplomats in Argentina, Canada, Haiti, Peru, and Spain.[7]

Police never identified the person who letter-bombed Boston's Government Center in March 1971, but attention soon refocused on the Middle East, where Palestinian terrorists mimicked the Zionist tactic of mailbombing. Between December 1971 and April 1973, at least 231 bombs related to Middle Eastern conflicts were mailed to targets on six continents, killing one person and wounding at least 10. Eight bombs sent to Palestinian activists may have indicated strife between rival militant groups, or may have represented retaliation by Israel.[8]

The Provisional Irish Republican Army began letter-bombing in May 1972, mailing at least 68 charges to various targets through December 1979. All but one, which went to the United States, were mailed to targets in England and Ireland. At least 42 persons were injured by explosions during that campaign.[9]

Other mail-bombing terrorists from the 1970s remain unidentified today. In Zambia they struck a Chinese embassy and Zambia's Ministry of Information during the summer of 1973. In May 1974 bomb-squad experts from the Metropolitan Police Department of Washington, D.C., disarmed a mail bomb at the Peruvian embassy. Six months later, in Australia, a letter bomb addressed to Queensland Premier Joh Bjelke-Petersen injured two clerks, while police experts defused another sent to Prime Minister Malcolm Fraser. In June 1976 16 letter bombs were sent from Texas to companies across the United States following extortion letters from an unknown criminal who signed the notes "B.F. Fox." During February and March 1977 apparent Puerto Rican nationalists sent mail bombs to President James Carter and three Manhattan banks. Two different groups, the Jewish Action Movement and the International Committee Against Nazism, claimed credit for five mail bombs sent to neo-Nazis across the United States in June 1979.[10]

More recent mail bombings betray a mixture of insanity and politics. "Unabomber" Theodore Kaczynski set the tone, mimicked by Austrian racist Franz Fuchs, who killed four victims and wounded 15 with 23 mail bombs sent during 1993–95. (Sentenced to life imprisonment in 1999, Fuchs hanged himself in jail.) In 1996 Icelandic singer Björk escaped injury when a deranged fan mailed her an acid bomb. In January 1997 seven letter bombs were mailed from Egypt to international officers of *Al-Hayat*, an Arabic newspaper.[11]

The 21st century brought no end to mail bombings. Beginning in 2005 a terrorist who called himself "The Bishop" wrote to various U.S. financial institutions demanding that they raise their stock prices to $6.66—the Biblical "Number of the Beast" from *Revelation* 13:16-18. None complied, and two companies received mail bombs without detonators in January 2007, accompanied by further threats. Four months later, U.S. postal inspectors arrested Iowa resident John Patrick Tomkins on 15 federal charges. A judge dismissed 10 of these charges in March 2009, but one month later, prosecutors filed a 13-count indictment against Tomkins based on a new grand jury's findings. As this book went to press, his trial had not been held.

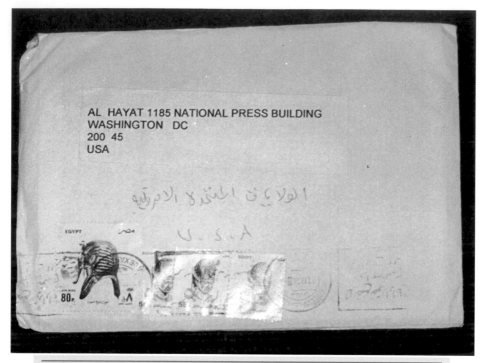

AL HAYAT 1185 NATIONAL PRESS BUILDING
WASHINGTON DC
200 45
USA

الولايات المتح\ة الامريكيه

U. S. A

EGYPT

80₽

In January 1997 at least 14 letter bombs were sent to the *Al-Hayat* headquarters in London and its bureaus in New York, Riyadh, and Washington, D.C. The perpetrator was never found. *(Bettmann/ Corbis)*

Elsewhere, in August 2007, Canadian police charged Lebanese immigrant Adel Arnaout with mailing letter bombs to three persons whom he felt had obstructed his plans to become an actor. Radical animal activists have also resorted to mail bombs. December 2008 saw a mail bomb sent to Elise Weerts, whose research at Johns Hopkins University includes experiments on monkeys. A letter signed by the Animal Liberation Brigade claimed credit for this and another mailing (not received), which was addressed to Steven Hsiao, another Johns Hopkins researcher.[12]

DETECTING MAIL BOMBS

While anyone may theoretically receive mail bombs from mentally unbalanced enemies, controversial public figures are at special risk.

MILES COOPER

Over a three-week period in early 2007, Britain suffered a series of seven mail bombings that injured a total of nine victims. The first three bombs were sent to forensic laboratories in Abingdon, Chelmsley Wood, and Culham. One envelope bore the name of Barry Horne (1952–2001), an animal-rights activist who died in prison while serving an 18-year sentence for firebombing stores that sold animal products. Police naturally suspected that the bombs were mailed by extremist admirers of Horne.

That theory started to crumble on February 3, when a mail bomb exploded at Mike Wingfield's home in Folkestone, leaving him with multiple wounds. The bomb was addressed to Wingfield as senior manager of a defunct security firm he once ran from his home, which had no link to animal testing.

(continues)

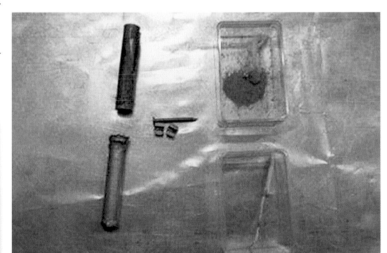

Prosecutors used the remains of a device sent to LGC Forensics as part of their case against Miles Cooper, who was found guilty of carrying out a nationwide letter bomb campaign in England in which eight people were injured. *(Associated Press)*

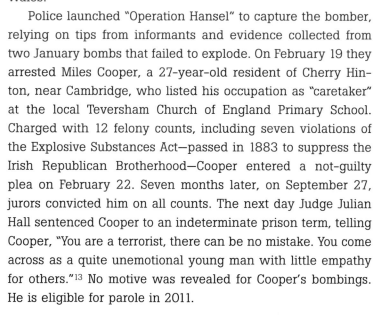

(continued)

Three more bombs exploded between February 5 and 7, none addressed to labs. The first injured an employee at London's Capital Centre, a firm that collects fees from drivers in the city's downtown Congestion Charge Zone. On February 6 another bomb wounded two employees at the Vantis accounting firm in Workingham, which housed the offices of Speed Check Services, a manufacturer of digital cameras for traffic police. The final bomb, on February 7, hospitalized four workers from the Driver and Vehicle Licensing Agency in Swansea, Wales.

Police launched "Operation Hansel" to capture the bomber, relying on tips from informants and evidence collected from two January bombs that failed to explode. On February 19 they arrested Miles Cooper, a 27-year-old resident of Cherry Hinton, near Cambridge, who listed his occupation as "caretaker" at the local Teversham Church of England Primary School. Charged with 12 felony counts, including seven violations of the Explosive Substances Act—passed in 1883 to suppress the Irish Republican Brotherhood—Cooper entered a not-guilty plea on February 22. Seven months later, on September 27, jurors convicted him on all counts. The next day Judge Julian Hall sentenced Cooper to an indeterminate prison term, telling Cooper, "You are a terrorist, there can be no mistake. You come across as a quite unemotional young man with little empathy for others."[13] No motive was revealed for Cooper's bombings. He is eligible for parole in 2011.

They—or, more often, their security personnel—learn to watch for suspicious packages and envelopes. The warning signs of a potential mail bomb may include the following:

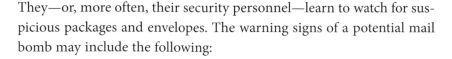

- No visible return address, or a suspicious listed source
- Errors in the delivery address, such as misspellings, incorrect titles, etc.

- Postmarks from a city different from that on the return address
- Items addressed with titles ("Manager," "Chief," etc.) but without a name
- Restrictive notations, such as "Personal" or "Confidential," meant to make the target open the package
- Excessive postage, often added to avoid having postal workers weigh the bomb
- Excessive string or tape used to secure a parcel's wrapping
- A package of unusual size, weight, or shape, including bulges or soft spots
- A lopsided, rigid, or lumpy envelope
- Any peculiar stains, smells, or protruding objects such as wire, string, or tinfoil
- Any peculiar sounds emerging from the parcel (buzzing, ticking, liquid sloshing, etc.)

A suspicious parcel should not be opened or handled beyond the bare minimum required to place it in a safe location. While Hollywood films often depict mail bombs being immersed in water, soaking may trigger some detonators. Once the package has been isolated, its recipient should take no further action beyond notifying U.S. postal inspectors and the nearest law enforcement agency, which will arrange for safe collection and disposal of the item.

Suspected mail bombs are often destroyed by police through various means, including gunfire or deliberate detonation inside a bomb-proof container. While such tactics may reveal a "false alarm," the toll of victims killed and injured by mail bombs since the 18th century dictates that safety take priority over possible embarrassment.

Bomb Squad Fatalities

Musa Qala, Afghanistan

Gary "Gaz" O'Donnell, a soldier in the British army's Royal Logistics Corps' elite bomb-disposal team, was a legend whose exploits rivaled anything portrayed in Hollywood fiction. Born in 1968, O'Donnell joined the army at age 23 and served three peaceful tours of duty at ammunition depots before he was posted to Northern Ireland. In 2006 he was transferred to southern Iraq, where he earned the George Medal for "acts of great bravery."[1]

O'Donnell's specific citation praised him for "showing selflessness and composure in challenging and distressing situations." It went on to say: "He has demonstrated consistent bravery in rendering safe devices intended to kill and maim by a highly sophisticated enemy. It is without question that he saved lives whilst risking his own and is worthy of true recognition."[2]

O'Donnell explained his work to BBC News, noting that while many UXBs are disarmed by robots such as the "wheelbarrow," conditions in Iraq often rendered such equipment useless. "Unfortunately," said O'Donnell, "with the dust, the sand, the heat, and the landscape, we didn't always have that remote capability. The wheelbarrow couldn't get to where it was needed or it was only lasting a few minutes or so because motors would overheat."[3] That left O'Donnell to go in alone, defusing the charges by hand.

Following his decoration ceremony in London, O'Donnell shipped out to Afghanistan. The change excited him. As he told BBC News, "The devices are different. The groups are different. So there are a whole lot of challenges out there that I can't wait to rise to."[4]

One such was the IED that O'Donnell was called to disarm in Helmand Province during June 2008. The device was patched together from an 82mm mortar shell and a 107mm rocket, containing five pounds of high explosives altogether. Its trigger was fashioned from a wooden clothespin and a rubber band. O'Donnell knelt over the bomb, prepared to clip its wires, when something went wrong.

"I saw the ends of the peg moving," he later explained. "I didn't have time to think. I had to act straightaway. I just jammed my fingers in. If I hadn't done it, if it had shut, I wouldn't be here."[5]

Skill and luck saved Gaz O'Donnell's life that day, but his luck ran out two months later. On September 10, 2008, he was called to disarm an IED found by soldiers outside Musa Qala, but the bomb exploded before he could reach it; the blast killed O'Donnell instantly. Investigators believe it was booby-trapped with an anti-handling device that earlier searches had missed.

O'Donnell left a wife and four children ranging in age from nine weeks to 16 years. While they mourned his loss, his commander credited O'Donnell with saving thousands of lives by disarming IEDs in Northern Ireland, the Falkland Islands, Germany, Sierra Leone, Iraq, and Afghanistan.[6]

OFFICERS DOWN

Considering the number of bombings and attempted bombings throughout America's history—3,814 during 2004–07 alone, with 15 persons killed and 135 injured—it is rather surprising that only 30 American police officers have died in bomb blasts since the first fatal attack in 1886. More remarkable still, only five of the 30 were killed while attempting to disarm explosive devices.[7] Those slain by bombs during the course of normal duty include the following:

- *May 4, 1886*: During a labor rally at Chicago's Haymarket Square, an unknown person hurled a bomb at police, killing Patrolmen

John Barrett, Mathias Degan, Nels Hansen, and George Miller. During the riot that followed, four more officers and at least four civilians were killed. Prosecutors charged eight alleged anarchists with murder. At trial in June 1886, all were convicted; seven were sentenced to hang, while two received 15-year prison terms. Four of the condemned were executed, while a fifth committed suicide in jail. Six years later, Illinois Governor John Altgeld pardoned the survivors, declaring his belief that all eight were innocent. The bomb-thrower remains unidentified.[8]

○ *October 1, 1907*: Sheriff Harvey Brown died in the explosion of a bomb rigged to the front door of his home in Baker County, Oregon. While the crime remains unsolved, investigators thought Sheriff Brown was slain for his part in the February 1906 arrest of Harry Orchard, who murdered former governor Frank Steunenberg with a bomb at *his* home in December 1905.

○ *November 24, 1917*: Two boys found a bomb outside a church in Milwaukee, Wisconsin, and carried it to police headquarters. There, it exploded while being examined, killing Station Keeper Henry Deckert and six officers: Frederick Kaiser, David O'Brien, Charles Seehawer, Edward Spindler, Stephen Stecker, and Albert Templin. Anarchists were blamed for the explosion, but no suspects were identified.

○ *March 1, 1925*: Inspector Orville Preuster, employed by the U.S. Customs Service in New York City, died in the explosion of a bomb wired to his car's ignition switch. Although the crime remains unsolved, authorities suspect that he was killed for his efforts to stop liquor smuggling across the Canadian border.

○ *November 9, 1925*: Unknown assassins lobbed a bomb into the Chicago home of Patrolman Frederick Schmitz, leaving him dead in the wreckage. Detectives surmised that Schmitz was killed "in retaliation for his police work," but no specific case was cited and the killer remains unknown.[9]

○ *February 16, 1928*: Chief of Police James Welch led a liquor raid outside of Lewisberry, Pennsylvania, and was injured when the booby-trapped still (an apparatus used in the distillation of alcohol) exploded. Welch's injuries combined with ill effects from a year-old gunshot wound to claim his life on February 23.

- *November 16, 1964*: Patrolman John Clowar and his partner answered a call involving a man who had threatened to blow up a tavern in Trenton, New Jersey. As the officers approached, the suspect detonated a hand grenade he was holding. The blast killed Patrolman Clowar, the grenade wielder, and a civilian bystander.
- *February 16, 1970*: An IED exploded inside the San Francisco Police Department's Park Station in Golden Gate Park. Sergeant Brian McDonnell suffered injuries that claimed his life two days later. The crime remains unsolved, but authorities suspect that the bomb was planted by members of the Weather Underground Organization (WUO), a radical group that declared war on the U.S. government in May 1970. Authorities blame the WUO for 22 bombings and two bombing attempts between October 1969 and July 1975, although group spokesmen did not claim their first "official" bombing until June 1970, three months after the accidental detonation of a New York "bomb factory" killed three WUO members. A federal grand jury indicted several Weathermen on explosives charges in July 1970, but the case was dismissed in October 1973.[10]
- *August 17, 1970*: At 2:23 A.M. police in Omaha, Nebraska, answered an anonymous report of screams from an abandoned house. When they went inside, a suitcase exploded, killing Officer Larry Minard and injuring seven others. Detectives identified 15-year-old Duane Peak as the 911 caller, and recorded various contradictory statements from him. They finally settled on Black Panther Party members Edward Poindexter and David Rice as the bombers. Both received life prison terms, but persons linked to their defense harbor troubling suspicions about Peak's role in the case. Nebraska's Parole Board has repeatedly suggested commutations of both sentences since 1993, but the separate Board of Pardons refuses to cooperate.[11]
- *January 13, 1972*: Would-be robber Fred Hokenson entered a drugstore in Lewiston, Idaho, armed with an IED and a knife. Officers Ross Flavel and Tom Saleen arrested Hokenson at the scene, but his bomb exploded in Flavel's hands, killing the officer instantly. Hokenson received a life sentence for murder.

(Continues on page 62)

HAZARDOUS DUTY ROBOTS

Bomb squad officers use any tools available to make their jobs safer. Remotely controlled vehicles (RCVs) have been used in IED disposal since March 1972, when Lieutenant Colonel Peter Miller introduced the "Wheelbarrow" to cope with bombs in Northern Ireland. A tracked vehicle controlled by radio signals, the Wheelbarrow passed through 10 revised models between its introduction and 2003, when the latest version went to war in Iraq. By the time newer machines began replacing Wheelbarrows in 2007, more than 400 had been destroyed by bomb blasts, each one representing an officer's life that was spared by technology.[12]

The Wheelbarrow's replacement in Britain was the six-wheeled Northrup Grumman Cutlass, which featured a more sophisticated gripper arm with a maximum reach of 8 feet and 2 inches (versus the Wheelbarrow's 5 feet and 3 inches). The Cutlass can move objects weighing up to 44 pounds and can outclass the Wheelbarrow—also built by Northrup Grumman—on a wide variety of terrain.[13]

Other robots designed for hazardous duty—extending beyond IED disposal to intervention during armed hostage situations and penetration of areas contaminated by deadly radioactive, chemical, or biological materials—include the following:

★ The Mini-Andros is a two-tracked RCV measuring 35 inches long, 16 inches wide, and 30.5 inches tall, with movable arms that enable it to climb stairs, cross small ditches, and perform other difficult maneuvers. Its grasping arm is capable of lifting 15 pounds and is smaller than that of the Cutlass, with a 24-inch horizontal reach and a 36-inch vertical extension. It carries low-light video cameras, plus a 12-gauge shotgun, high-pressure water cannon, and a charge-dropper for *delivering* explosives. Its top speed is 70 feet per minute. The price tag: $40,000 to $60,000.[14]

★ The Robug III was developed by British inventors who first studied crabs and spiders. This RCV travels on eight 39-inch legs that support a "body" measuring 31 inches long, 24 inches wide, and 24 inches high. Its unique mode of travel lets the robot step over obstacles that could block wheeled or tracked models, and its vacuum-gripper "feet" allow Robug III to climb vertical walls, including those built of rough bricks. On retrieval missions, it can drag objects weighing up to 221 pounds at a top speed of 20 feet per minute. The price tag: $1.3 million.[15]

★ The STAR (Spiral Track Autonomous Robot) employs another unique means of travel. The STAR derives its "spiral track" name from two screws—one left-hand and one right-hand—which propel it along the ground, rotating in different directions to move the robot forward, backward, left, or right, and rotating clockwise or counter-clockwise while standing in

(continues)

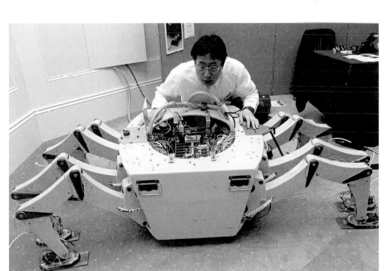

Dr. Bing Luk crouches over his creation, the ROBUG III, at the Royal Society in London in June 1996. The machine was being previewed in the "New Frontiers in Science" exhibition. *(Associated Press)*

(continued)

place. This system lets the STAR navigate rocky, sandy, or muddy terrain, and because the screws are hollow, it may also cross waterlogged ground, streams, and rivers. The STAR, which is 38 inches square and 30 inches high, can travel 20 feet per minute when moving forward or backward, and 133 feet per minute when moving sideways. As with the other robots, the STAR may carry a variety of cameras, microphones, infrared sensors, gas and radiation sensors, plus a micropower impulse radar landmine detection device. The relatively modest price tag: $15,000.[16]

(Continued from page 59)

- *February 14, 1974*: Night-prowling killers lobbed a firebomb into the Hazel Township, Pennsylvania, home of Deputy Sheriff Eugene Boyarski, killing Boyarski, his wife, and three children. Detectives identified local residents James Mastrota and James Sandutch as the bombers in September 1974. Both were later convicted of murder and arson, received life terms, and died in prison.

- *March 2, 1976*: Armed with a shotgun and a suitcase filled with dynamite, Bruce Sisk entered the Mason County Jail in Point Pleasant, West Virginia, to liberate his wife, who was being held on a charge of killing their two-year-old child. Sisk reached his wife's cell before Sheriff Elvin Wedge fired a shot that struck the suitcase, which exploded. The blast killed Sisk, his wife, and Deputy Sheriff Kenneth Love. Sheriff Wedge died from his injuries on March 3, followed by jailer Ernest Hesson on March 9.

- *May 2, 1979*: A mail bomb addressed to the newly elected public safety commissioner of Bessemer, Alabama, exploded when Lieutenant Clifford Hill opened the package. The bomb killed Hill and injured a secretary. Investigators blamed the crime on an ex-policeman whose plans to become chief of police were spoiled by the new commissioner's election. Confused reports of the trial's outcome—claiming both conviction *and* acquittal of the suspect— were unresolved as this book went to press.[17]

- *February 15, 1990*: Detective Dennis Wustenhoff died when a bomb demolished his car outside his home in Patchogue, New York. The case remains unsolved.

- *October 28, 1991*: Officer Jeremiah Hurley Jr. responded to a call concerning a suspicious package at the Boston home of Thomas Shay. The bomb, which had dislodged from underneath Shay's car, exploded as Hurley examined it, killing him and wounding Officer Francis Foley. Shay's son, Thomas Jr., named Alfred Trenkler as the bomb-maker. Trenkler pled guilty and received a life sentence, which was later reduced on appeal. Jurors convicted Shay's son of conspiracy in 1993, resulting in a 15-year sentence.

- *February 1, 1992*: Paul Howell, a Florida man facing charges for drug dealing, planned to kill his ex-wife with a bomb hidden inside a gift-wrapped microwave oven, thus preventing her from testifying against him in court. While en route to her house, with a friend driving the car, Howell was stopped in Jefferson County by State Trooper James Fulford Jr. After arresting Howell and his companion on unrelated charges, Fulford examined the package and died when it exploded in his hands. Howell was condemned in 1995 and remains on death row today. His driver received a 40-year sentence.

- *January 29, 1998*: A bomb planted by Eric Rudolph exploded at a women's clinic in Birmingham, Alabama, killing a nurse and Officer Sande Sanderson. Rudolph's guilty pleas for various crimes in 2005 included this bombing. He received five consecutive life sentences.

- *December 12, 2008*: Two banks in Woodburn, Oregon, received telephoned bomb threats, bringing police to each scene. A package found at the first bank proved harmless, but a bomb at the second location exploded while police examined it, killing State Trooper William Hakim and Captain Tom Tennant of the Woodburn Police Department and injuring Woodburn Police Chief Scott Russell. On December 19 authorities charged 57-year-old Bruce Turnidge and his son, 32-year-old Joshua Turnidge, of planting the fatal bomb. As this book went to press, a trial was scheduled for September 2010, and a judge ruled in March 2010 that the state could seek the death penalty.

FALLEN HEROES

Statistics testify to the success of America's IED-disposal experts. From 2004 to 2007, when 3,814 bombing attacks and attempts were recorded,

CANINE CASUALTIES

Humans are not the only species that risks death for the sake of IED disposal. Dogs have been used for many years to sniff out various kinds of contraband, including drugs, illegal weapons, and explosives. They are used by police and military bomb squads alike, often sent into places where humans feel unsafe despite their advanced training and protective gear.

 At Holsworthy Army Barracks in Sydney, Australia, a monument to martyred bomb–disposal dogs stands beside the Explosive Ordinance Disposal Training Centre, where soldiers learn to disarm IEDs and UXBs. Next door is the School of Military Engineering, where chosen dogs are trained for 18 months before deployment in the field. The memorial honors three dogs killed on duty in Afghanistan: Merlin (August 31, 2007), Razz (September 30, 2007), and Andy (November 23, 2007).

Major Jason Eltham, in charge of the camp's Specialized Engineering Wing, explains why dogs are so useful in IED retrieval: "Their ability is way in excess of any other explosive detection capability in an open field, a room, or a car." Sergeant Damian Dunne, one of the school's expert trainers, adds that while every dog has a keen nose, IED work requires "frantic retrievers" whose performance justifies the $80,000 cost of training that prepares a dog for an average of six years' active service.[18]

Police and military dogs all over the world share hazardous tasks with their human masters. In February 2007 the U.S. Transportation Security Administration alone employed more

none of the 15 persons killed and 135 injured were bomb-squad officers.[19] Still, there *have* been casualties, and those fallen heroes deserve
mention here.

- Detectives Joseph Lynch and Ferdinand Socha were members of
  the NYPD bomb squad. On July 4, 1940, they were summoned
  to the British Pavilion at the World's Fair in Flushing Meadows,

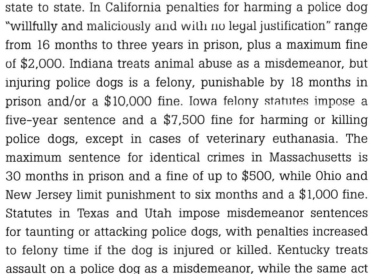

than 9,000 dogs to patrol 75 airports and 13 major transit
systems.[20] Many more work for other federal, state, and local
agencies. One published report lists 39 police dogs killed on
active duty in the United States and Canada between 1980
and 2000, prompting passage of protective laws in at least
12 states. In August 2000 Congress also passed the Federal
Law Enforcement Animal Protection Act, imposing a one-year
prison term on anyone who harms or conspires to harm any
police animal. If the animal dies or suffers permanent disability, the sentence may increase to 10 years.[21]

The local approach to protecting police dogs varies from
state to state. In California penalties for harming a police dog
"willfully and maliciously and with no legal justification" range
from 16 months to three years in prison, plus a maximum fine
of $2,000. Indiana treats animal abuse as a misdemeanor, but
injuring police dogs is a felony, punishable by 18 months in
prison and/or a $10,000 fine. Iowa felony statutes impose a
five-year sentence and a $7,500 fine for harming or killing
police dogs, except in cases of veterinary euthanasia. The
maximum sentence for identical crimes in Massachusetts is
30 months in prison and a fine of up to $500, while Ohio and
New Jersey limit punishment to six months and a $1,000 fine.
Statutes in Texas and Utah impose misdemeanor sentences
for taunting or attacking police dogs, with penalties increased
to felony time if the dog is injured or killed. Kentucky treats
assault on a police dog as a misdemeanor, while the same act
ranks as a felony in Florida and Missouri.[22]

Detective Arleigh McCree of the Los Angeles Police Department Bomb Squad handles "Fearless Felix," the squad's new robot, in 1984. McCree, a respected explosives expert, was killed two years later while trying to disarm two pipe bombs. *(Associated Press)*

Queens, to remove a suspected time bomb. They found a suitcase on the building's third floor and heard ominous ticking sounds from inside. Detective Lynch carried the bag outside, opened it, and died with Socha in the resultant blast, which also injured two other policemen. Speculation focused on Nazi saboteurs, since Britain had declared war on Germany 10 months earlier, but 1939 and 1940 also witnessed multiple IRA bombings in Britain. The crime remains unsolved today. NYPD bomb experts soon began using X-rays to examine suspicious parcels, and acquired their first "total containment vehicle," a flatbed truck with a container woven from steel cables left over from construction of the Brooklyn Bridge in 1883.[23]

- Officer Angel Cordero-Roman served on the Puerto Rico Police Department, which has been considered an American law enforcement agency since the United States seized Puerto Rico from Spain in 1898. On August 28, 1961, Officer Corder-Roman died in the explosion of an IED he was attempting to disarm at the police lab in San Juan. The bomb-maker remains unidentified.
- Detective Arleigh McCree and Officer Ronald Ball, members of the Los Angeles Police Department's bomb squad, were summoned to deactivate two pipe bombs found at a private home on February 18, 1986. As they attempted to disarm the IEDs, one exploded, killing Detective McCree instantly and fatally wounding Officer Ball. McCree was a world-renowned IED expert. He participated in the 1983 investigation of a suicide bombing that killed 242 American servicemen in Lebanon. Later, he rejected a job offer from Libyan dictator Muammar al-Gaddafi, who asked McCree to teach terrorists the art of bomb making.

While IEDs continue to kill military experts such as Gary O'Donnell on foreign battlefields, more than two decades have elapsed since the last bomb-squad officer's death in America. That record testifies to their expertise in one of law enforcement's most dangerous jobs.

Explosives Detection

Barrow, Alaska

In May 2007 Inuit tribesmen killed a 50-ton bowhead whale off the coast of Alaska in a hunt approved by their treaties with the U.S. government. While butchering the whale for meat and blubber, they found a 3.5-inch metal fragment embedded in one of the whale's shoulder blades. Experts identified the conical object as part of an explosive projectile invented in 1879 and manufactured until 1885. The projectile had exploded, but it obviously failed to kill its intended prey. Based on the conclusion that professional whalers would not have tried to kill an immature calf, marine biologists speculated that the bowhead whale must have been 115 to 130 years old when its luck finally ran out.[1]

Four months after that surprising discovery, in September 2007, police in Ogden, Utah, responded to a bomb scare at Weber State University. No IED was found on campus, but the school's resident bomb-detection dog, Balou, led officers to a nearby private home where an illegal cache of blasting caps was found in a closet. Balou sniffed them out, despite the fact that they were sealed inside an air-tight Tupperware container. Officers arrested the home's resident, 31-year-old Raymond Guzman, on charges of stealing the caps and other explosive material from a storage shed in Layton. Also charged were Curtis Beeman (who allegedly phoned in the campus bomb threat) and Raymond Bradley Parr (an employee at Hill Air Force Base who illegally stored the material before Guzman and Beeman stole it).

Police had finished searching Guzman's house before they put Balou to work, and he found the hidden items they had overlooked. Balou's handler, Corporal Dennis Moore, told reporters that the German shepherd enjoyed his outing. "It's fun for him to get out and work," Moore said.[2]

And in the process, he saves lives.

SPOTTING BOMBS

Detection of an IED is the first vital step toward disarming it, and it may be a difficult task. Without a smoking fuse, a ticking clock, or a bomber thoughtful enough to tell police where he planted the charge, officers have to look for themselves. But where should they look? And at what?

The earliest form of IED/UXB detection involved a simple metal detector, patented by inventor Gerhard Fisher in 1937 and used for the first time to locate landmines during World War II. Metal detectors still play a prominent role in battlefield mine clearance, but wooden and plastic mine casings required new techniques for location of hidden charges.

One such method is ground-penetrating radar (GPR), which uses electromagnetic radiation in the radio spectrum's super high frequency range to locate objects buried or implanted in various materials, including soil, ice, concrete, limestone, and granite. GPR detection requires no metal components, but several companies now manufacture a hybrid system that combines ground-penetrating radar with more traditional metal detection for maximum efficiency.

German physicist Wilhelm Röntgen revolutionized medical science when he discovered X-rays in 1895, and while some police departments used X-rays to examine suspected IEDs over the next 30 years, X-ray machines did not become standard airport security equipment until the late 1960s. Various methods exist that rely on well-trained operators to spot IEDs that may include plastic explosives molded in the shape of common objects, but technological advances continue to make the job simpler. Dual-energy X-ray machines project two beams through luggage or parcels: one displays organic materials (food, leather, paper, etc.) in red, while inorganic objects (metal, plastic, etc.) show up in blue or green.

Other mechanical systems rival X-rays in detecting IEDs. Quadrupole resonance (QR) technology, for example, uses radio waves to depict the contents of closed containers, revealing bombs, other weapons, and illicit drugs. QR systems have also shown promise in landmine detection.[3]

Another IED-detection method borrowed from medical science is computed tomography (CT). It was invented in the early 1900s and adapted for scanning the human body by British researcher Godfrey Hounsfield in 1972, earning Hounsfield the 1979 Nobel Prize for Medicine. In CT scans, rotating X-rays scan the body or other object and computers analyze the resultant images.

In 1886 German physicist Eugen Goldstein discovered anode rays, beams of positive ions whose movement in low-pressure gas discharges may be tracked in vacuum tubes. Thus was born mass spectrometry, a technique for determining chemical composition of various unknown materials. Modern systems include ion mobility spectrometery (used to identify very low concentrations of chemicals), differential mobility spectrometry (presenting fewer false-positive results, also capable of identifying bacteria species), chemiluminescence (detecting emission of light or heat from chemical compounds), and amplifying fluorescent polymer sensors (which "turn off" the fluorescence of specifically selected chemical molecules). All are used today to recognize different explosives.

Another mechanical technique, neutron activation analysis (NAA), involves bombardment of a suspect material with neutron radiation, which in turn causes measurable radioactivity in various materials. Used extensively by forensic scientists, NAA is an extremely accurate method of identifying trace elements, even when concealed within a larger mass of disparate material.

MECHANICAL "NOSES"

Many chemicals, including explosives, have distinctive smells. Some scents are easily detected—the early plastic explosive Nobel 808 smelled like almonds; modern Semtex smells like marzipan candy—but those may be disguised. Other compounds fail to register on human nostrils.

Machine olfaction uses various machines to simulate a living crea-ture's sense of smell. Some chemicals, like nitroglycerine, emit vapors that are easily detected by basic chemosensors ("sniffers"), while others, including some components of modern plastic explosives, require more sophisticated devices.

Development of "electronic noses" began in 1982 with the production of machines that could recognize basic scents and flavors. In recent years electronic sensing (or "e-sensing") technology has advanced by combin-ing elements of mass spectrometry with gas chromatography, a process that separates and identifies various chemicals within a compound by calculating their speed of movement within streams of gas or liquid.

An electronic nose consists of three parts: a sample delivery system, a sensor (detection) system, and a computing system. Delivery involves collection of samples by touch (as with swabs) or by "inhaling" invis-ible fumes. Most devices use an array of sensors, which react to contact with different volatile chemicals and experience changes in their own electronic properties. The most commonly used sensors include con-ducting polymers, field effect transistors, metal oxide semiconductors, quartz crystal microbalance devices, and surface acoustic wave systems. Finally, the machine's computer analyzes the collected data and identi-fies the various chemicals detected, assigning digital values based on statistical models.[4]

LIVING TOOLS

Many experts in the field of IED/UXB detection still prefer to trust a liv-ing nose whenever possible. Dogs are the most common species used to track explosives, but their special training may cost $80,000, in addition to support during their working lives and salaries paid to dog handlers.[5] "Scent hounds"—as opposed to "sight hounds" that rely primarily on vision—have been used for centuries to hunt animals and humans, including fugitive criminals, but training for explosives detection began in 1970 with Charles Kirchner, a dog handler for the Metropolitan Police Department in Washington, D.C. Retired in 1980 after 20 years of active duty, Kirchner now runs Charles Kirchner Canine Consultants Inc., training dogs at a facility in South Carolina.[6]

(Continues on page 74)

BOMB-SNIFFING BEES

No one knows exactly when humans "discovered" honey, but rock art dating from 13,000 B.C. depicts tribal honey gathering, and organized *apiculture* (beekeeping) is documented from ancient Egypt, Greece, and Rome. It was not until the 21st century, however, that *entomologists* (scientists who study insects) discovered yet another use for honey bees: detecting hidden explosives.

In December 2003 the Mine Action Information Center at Virginia's James Madison University reported efforts to train bomb-sniffing bees at several U.S. laboratories (efforts were bankrolled by the Defense Advanced Research Project Agency's (DARPA) Controlled Biological and Biomimetic Systems Program). According to DARPA, tests conducted during 2001–02 demonstrated that bees could detect small quantities of the explosive dinitrotoluene when it was mixed with sand. Further tests done at Missouri's Fort Leonard Wood in July and August 2003 appeared to confirm those findings, but the Mine Action Information Center declared that "many of these reports are inaccurate and may encourage individuals and demining groups to 'sell' a service that they poorly understand or lack the experience to properly apply."[7]

In November 2006 the story resurfaced, with journalists reporting that bees had been taught to detect IEDs in another program, conducted at New Mexico's Los Alamos National Laboratory. Trained with rewards of sugar water, the bees reportedly had learned to sniff out vapors released by dynamite, C4 plastic explosive, and triacetone triperoxide—all commonly worn by suicide bombers. Tim Haarmann, principal investigator for the lab's Stealthy Insect Sensor Project, told reporters, "Scientists have long marveled at the honey bee's phenomenal sense of smell, which rivals that of dogs. But previous attempts to harness and understand this ability were scientifically unproven. With more knowledge, our team thought we could make use of this ability."[8]

Experimentation with bees soon spread to Europe, where Professor Nikola Kezic conducted research at the University of Zagreb in Croatia. Kezic claimed that his bees could be trained in a matter of days for performance in tandem with humans bearing heat-sensitive cameras. The new technique, if successful, may be especially useful in Croatia, where some 250,000 mines planted during ethnic warfare in the 1990s remain in a region spanning 380 square miles.[9]

A researcher straps a bomb-sniffing honey bee into a custom-designed harness before a training session. Researchers are taking advantage of bees' keen sense of smell and their love of nectar to produce an effective means of bomb detection. *(Getty Images)*

(Continued from page 71)

Despite their familiarity and widespread use in law enforcement, dogs are not the only mammals trained to locate explosive devices.

● Gambian pouched rats are African rodents that rival small raccoons in size, with an average weight approaching nine pounds. Their docile personality and keen sense of smell permit these rats to be trained in landmine detection through food-reward incentives, while their relatively light weight prevents them from detonating mines on contact. Most are trained by scientists in Belgium (which once owned Africa's Congo region). Ongoing experiments

A U.S. Marine puts his bomb-sniffing dog near a roadside bomb while anti-explosives squad members finalize details before blowing it up. *(AFP/Getty Images)*

with electrode implants suggest that it may someday be possible for people to guide pouched rats as "ratbots" into places inaccessible to humans.[10]

o Dwarf mongooses are carnivores native to African grasslands, where they rarely exceed 11 inches in length or 12 ounces in weight. Thrishantha Nanayakkara, an engineer at Sri Lanka's University of Moratuwa, trains dwarf mongooses to find landmines by smell (guided by a remote-controlled robot).[11] As with the giant pouched rat, that skill could theoretically extend to IEDs planted in other settings.

o Pigs are trained by ex-Israeli soldier Giva Zin for work detecting landmines. As an army dog handler, Zin noted that while dogs did well at locating mines planted in shallow pits, they often missed others placed in deeper holes. Pigs naturally root for food and can be trained to recognize the smell of various explosive compounds. Ironically, Zin says, "Jews don't like pigs. Even Jews who are not religious have a strong aversion to pigs." Therefore, he adds, "This project is not for Israel. It is for places like Angola."[12]

o Dolphins and sea lions are trained by the U.S. Navy to detect sea mines lying on or tethered to the ocean floor. Enemy mines claimed 14 of the 19 U.S. military vessels sunk or damaged since 1950, which makes this research project high-priority. In addition to detecting mines, marine mammals can also attach markers to their tether lines and help human divers chart safe corridors for delivery of troops during amphibious landings.[13]

Mammals are not the only creatures suitable for use in explosive detection. Insects dominate the earth by sheer numbers and diversity of species, but not all are pests. Honeybees are also trained to sniff out explosives, and research continues with other insect species, including certain moths.[14]

A bacterium known as a bioreporter, genetically engineered to produce a measurable signal in response to contact with specific chemicals or physical agents, may also be used to detect explosives. As in other experiments, the original tests have focused on landmines planted in open countryside, where bacteria can be sprayed over large areas. A reaction to explosives in the form of color changes may save hours or days of human searching for buried charges, but some false-positive results have been logged around water and various plants. So far, bacteria have proved reliable for detecting small amounts of TNT, but research on plastic explosives remains ongoing.[15]

Even plants may be used to detect landmines. Specifically, the weed thale cress—a member of the mustard family, which grows wild

WAS THAT A BOMB?

Forensic scientists are often asked to determine whether a deadly blast was accidental or an act of terrorism. Two modern airline tragedies illustrate the methods involved.

On July 17, 1996, Trans World Airlines Flight 800 left New York's John F. Kennedy Airport, bound for Paris with 212 passengers and 18 crew members. Soon after takeoff, at 8:31 P.M., the plane exploded over the Atlantic Ocean, killing everyone on board. Agents of the FBI and the National Transportation Safety Board (NTSB) interviewed 736 witnesses to the tragedy. Of those, 599 reported a "fireball" in the sky, while 210 claimed they had seen a "streak of light" rise from the ocean's surface toward the aircraft before it exploded.[16]

While terrorism was suspected—either in the form of an IED smuggled aboard the plane or a rocket fired from a boat below—analysis of Flight 800's wreckage attributed the explosion to a freak accident involving a malfunction in the jet's fuel tanks. Despite that official finding, many researchers still believe that the plane was shot down by terrorists and that U.S. officials concealed the evidence to avoid widespread panic.[17]

Eight years after Flight 800's destruction, on August 24, 2004, two Russian airliners took off from Moscow's Domodedovo International Airport. Both subsequently crashed within

everywhere on Earth except the poles—has been genetically altered by Danish biologists Carsten Meier and Simon Østergaard to change colors when exposed to nitrous oxide (which commonly leaks out of mines underground). Field tests are still in progress, and while nitrous oxide naturally occurring in soil may produce false positives, scientists remain optimistic that thale cress may at least reduce the 10,000 persons killed or injured each year by landmines, while also trimming the $200 to $300 million spent yearly on mine retrieval.[18]

minutes of each other, at 10:56 and 10:59 P.M., killing a total of 89 people. Investigation by Russia's Federal Security Service revealed traces of the explosive RDX in wreckage from both aircraft, prompting the conclusion that "without a shadow of a doubt, both airplanes were blown up as a result of a terrorist attack."[19]

But by whom?

At the time of the bombings, Russian troops were battling Muslim guerrillas in the neighboring Chechen Republic. A Web site claiming to represent one such group, calling itself the Islambouli Brigades of al-Qaeda, took credit for both crashes, though it referred to hijackings and mentioned no bombings. In September 2004 Chechen rebel leader Shamil Basayev disputed the Islambouli Brigades's claims, announcing that he had hired the airplane bombers for 3,300 Euros ($4,000). Moscow police later named two Chechen women as suspected suicide bombers, acting to avenge the death of relatives at Russian hands. While they could not be tried and punished, police captain Mikhail Artamonov received a seven-year prison term for failing to search the women when he questioned them at the airport on the day of the crashes. An airline ticket agent, Armen Aratyunyan, also received an 18-month sentence for accepting false identification from both women before they boarded their flights.

TAGGANTS

Taggants are markers added to various materials for the purpose of identification or testing. Explosive taggants are divided into two broad categories: detection and identification. The first are used to help experts locate explosives prior to detonation, while the second type identifies explosive compounds after a blast, hopefully pinpointing their source and leading to the arrest of the bomb-makers.

While some explosives remain untagged today, the U.S. Antiterrorism Act of 1996 and the International Civil Aviation Organization's 1998 Convention on the Marking of Explosives for the Purpose of Identification demand insertion of both detection taggants (chemicals which slowly evaporate, emitting vapors detectable by trained animals or mechanical sensors) and identification taggants into all explosives.

In the United States, prevailing law requires use of the chemical taggant 2,3-dimethyl-2,3-dinitrobutane, generally known as DMNB. Both bomb-detection dogs and certain "electronic noses" are sensitive to DMNB at minute concentrations (down to .5 parts per billion in the air). Semtex plastic explosive, invented by Czech chemist Stanislav Brebera in the 1950s and commercially manufactured since 1964 for use worldwide, is generally tagged with ethylene glycol dinitrate (EGDN). Other chemical taggants used in foreign countries include mononitrotoluene (o-MNT) and para-mononitrotoluene (p-MNT), pale yellow chemicals with distinctive odors.

Identification taggants, by contrast, are typically physical objects designed to survive a bomb blast. Microscopic polymer particles are the most common, distinguished by their color and/or an imprinted code number traceable to a specific manufacturer. From there, since detailed records are required for all sales of explosives, investigators *should* be able to trace a particular shipment from factory to retail store, and on from there to individual buyers.

That system breaks down if explosives are stolen or if homemade explosives are used to build an IED. Noteworthy examples include the 1,500-pound car bomb made from urea nitrate-hydrogen gas, which killed six persons and injured 1,042 in the February 1993 World Trade Center bombing[20]; the April 1995 truck bomb containing 6,200 pounds of ammonium nitrate fertilizer, nitromethane, and diesel fuel that destroyed Oklahoma City's federal building, killing 168 persons and wounding over 800[21]; and the similar 500-pound car bomb that killed 29 victims and wounded more than 300 in Omagh, Northern Ireland, in August 1998.[22] Suspects were charged and convicted in all three cases, but investigators were forced to rely on informants and other evidence (damaged auto parts, etc.) to build their cases.

Rendered
Safe

London, England

At 1:25 A.M. on June 29, 2007, an ambulance team arrived on the scene of a minor car accident in London's Haymarket district, near Piccadilly Circus. Witnesses reported that the driver had crashed his Mercedes-Benz into a street-side trash bin, and then fled on foot. The ambulance attendants saw smoke rising from the car and called police, who cordoned off the block at 2 A.M. Inside the car, bomb-disposal experts found 16 gallons of gasoline, several cylinders of propane gas, and hundreds of nails meant to serve as shrapnel. They disarmed the bomb by hand at 3:30 A.M.

Meanwhile, traffic officers found another Mercedes parked nearby, illegally blocking traffic on Cockspur Street. They had it towed to a police impound lot at 3:30 A.M., where employees noted a strong smell of gasoline. Bomb squad officers found and disarmed an identical bomb in the second abandoned vehicle.

At 3:11 P.M. on June 30, two men crashed a Jeep Cherokee loaded with propane canisters into the glass doors of Scotland's Glasgow International Airport, then set the vehicle afire. The clumsy driver, Dr. Kafeel Ahmed, suffered major burns and was arrested at the scene with his companion, Dr. Bilal Abdullah. Five bystanders were slightly injured, while Ahmed—a Muslim born in India—died from his burns on August 2. Before his death, on July 1, bomb-squad officers executed a controlled explosion of a suspicious vehicle in the parking lot of the

Royal Alexandra Hospital, where Ahmed was confined. No bomb was found in that car.

By July 2 police had detained six other suspects in the botched bombing spree.

They included three more physicians—Dr. Sabeel Ahmed (Kafeel Ahmed's brother), Dr. Mohammed Haneef (a cousin of the Ahmed brothers, jailed in Australia), and Dr. Mohammed Asha—plus Dr. Asha's wife and two Saudi medical students whose names were not published. Asha's wife and the students were later released without charges, but jurors convicted Dr. Abdullah of conspiracy to commit murder, and he received a life prison term. Dr. Asha was acquitted in December 2008 and is presently resisting legal efforts to deport him from Britain. Detectives claimed that they found a subscriber identity module (SIM card) from Dr. Haneef's cell phone in the Glasgow Airport Jeep, but that statement proved false and Australian Federal Police cleared Haneef of all charges in August 2008.

MATTERS OF LIFE OR DEATH

Bomb disposal is the process by which explosive devices are rendered safe. The process as we know it today evolved during World War I, when soldiers disarmed landmines and "dud" bombs or artillery shells. The Ordnance Examiners of Britain's Royal Army Service Corps were the first true "bomb squad" experts, learning the job as they went along, without any specialized training or tools.

Explosive ordnance disposal (EOD) became more critical in World War II, when the Battle of Britain (1940–41) witnessed mass German bombings and rocket attacks against England. Many German bombs were fitted with time-delay fuses and anti-handling devices, such as the ZUS 40 anti-removal fuse, to increase panic among civilian populations and kill UXB-disposal experts. In 1941 the U.S. military supervised EOD training for members of the newly formed Office of Civilian Defense (OCD), with classes held at Maryland's Aberdeen Proving Ground. Trained initially by British experts, OCD members later received instruction from American officers such as Lieutenant Colonel Thomas Kane. Kane's best-known military graduates included Ronald Felton (active in Italy), Joseph Pilcher (in France and Germany), and

Richard Metress (in the Philippines). The job's danger was emphasized in 1945, when Metress and most of his 209th Bomb Disposal Squad died while disarming a Japanese IED. Worldwide, at least 40 U.S. EOD experts lost their lives between 1942 and 1945.[1]

The end of World War II coincided with the dawn of a new era of terrorism on all fronts, from distant lands to American soil. Bombers of all persuasions were confronted by both military EOD and IED disposal teams, and by the public safety bomb disposal (PSBD) squads attached to various police departments. British experts were led by ammunition technicians of the Royal Logistics Corps (serving in place of civilian police) to clear UXBs from London and IEDs from far-flung battle-grounds, including Palestine, Northern Ireland, Afghanistan, and Iraq.

Terrorist IEDs are not the only threat encountered by American bomb-disposal units, either. A November 2002 report from the Environmental Protection Agency found unexploded bombs or shells—including biological and chemical weapons—at 16,000 abandoned military sites across the United States, spanning nearly 40 million acres of land. Government expenses for disarming and removing UXO were estimated at a minimum of $14 billion, and perhaps "several times that."[2] The city of Orlando, Florida, canceled new building permits in December 2007, after construction workers found unexploded bombs from World War II near Odyssey Middle School. Even if old bombs, rockets, and shells do not explode, they pose a threat to the environment through leakage of various chemicals into the soil and water table.

UXO concerns are even greater in other nations, where ongoing warfare since the 1940s has left the globe littered with dangerous "duds." Examples include:

- *Vietnam*: The last foreign troops left this war-torn nation in 1975, but clean-up of the lethal mess they left behind continues. By 2000 more than 38,000 persons had been killed by abandoned landmines and UXO, with another 64,000 injured. During the same period, more than 4 million bombs and landmines were disarmed and removed, but 20 percent of the country remains contaminated, and deaths from UXO continue at a rate of 1,000 per year. In Quang Tri Province alone, an estimated 15 million landmines remain to be found and disarmed.[3]

- *Laos*: Vietnam's next-door neighbor suffered at least 520,000 U.S. air raids during the Vietnam War, depositing more than 5 million tons of bombs. Many of those were cluster bombs, each containing hundreds of deadly "bomblets." Ten of the 18 Laotian provinces are deemed "severely contaminated" with UXO (an estimated 9 million bombs altogether), which have killed or wounded at least 20,000 victims since 1975. America contributed $3.7 million toward removal of UXO in 2009 and plans to give $5 million in 2010.[4]

- *Lebanon*: Israel invaded its Arab neighbor on July 12, 2006, killing an estimated 1,191 Lebanese civilians and wounding more than 4,400 by October 1, when a cease-fire was declared. During the last days of the conflict, Israeli warplanes dropped tons of cluster bombs, making life perilous for Lebanese residents after Israeli troops withdrew. An estimated 1 million unexploded bombs still remain (1.5 bombs for each citizen of southern Lebanon). Two years later, following the death of United Nations demining expert Stefaan Vanpeteghem in September 2008, spokesmen for the U.N. Mine Action Coordination Center reported 258 deaths or injuries from UXO since the cease-fire. Worse yet, funds for the cleanup were nearly exhausted, according to center spokesperson Dalya Farran. She told the *Los Angeles Times* that the unit's budget for 2008 fell $4.7 million short of actual needs, adding that "2009 is a whole other story. Without funding, we will have to stop all the teams."[5]

- *Bosnia and Herzegovina*: More than a decade after brutal ethnic cleansing killed thousands in this Baltic state, UXO remains a daily peril. A total of 461,634 landmines had been destroyed by May 2004, with no end in sight. Even then, a total of 894 square miles were still described as "hazardous."[6]

RENDER SAFE PROCEDURES

Render safe procedures (RSP) are defined as "the application of special explosive ordnance disposal methods and tools to provide for the interruption of functions or separation of essential components to prevent an unacceptable detonation."[13] Active experts in the field often refuse

(Continues on page 86)

DEATH UNDERFOOT

Landmines are explosive devices, generally planted in or on the ground, to be detonated by remote control or upon physical contact with their intended targets. Their name derives from military "mining," wherein tunnels were dug beneath enemy camps or forts, then packed with explosives to wreak havoc on the surface. While ancient Romans dug spike-filled pits to wound enemy soldiers, the first explosive mines were apparently used by Chinese defenders against Mongol cavalry in A.D. 1277.[7]

Modern landmines are used for two main reasons: to secure borders or to limit enemy movements in an occupied territory. The problem is that unexploded mines remain when wars end, killing civilians for years afterward. Worldwide, between 1985 and 1995, International Red Cross hospitals treated 140,000 civilian war-wound victims, of whom 30,000 (21 percent) were injured by mines. According to Red Cross statistics, landmines kill or wound 26,000 victims each year, or one every 15 minutes.[8] Since 1997, 156 nations have ratified a Convention on the Prohibition of the Use, Stockpiling, Production and Transfer of Anti-Personnel Mines and on their Destruction, which bans production of anti-personnel mines (those meant to kill people). The countries still producing and planting landmines include the United States, China, India, Israel, Pakistan, and Russia.[9]

Demining or mine clearance is the process of removing mines that have been located through various techniques of minesweeping. In active combat zones, various rapid methods are employed, including carpet-bombing, burning the land with incendiaries such as napalm, or mine-clearing line charges such as the M58 "Giant Viper," a rocket-launched hose 350 feet long packed with five pounds of C4 plastic explosive per foot. If the impact of its landing in a minefield does not detonate nearby mines, operators can activate the C4 charges by remote control, using their shock waves to detonate mines. An alternate tool, jointly developed by the U.S. Army and Marine Corps, is the Anti-Personnel Obstacle Breaching System, which consists of a 125-pound unit that is hand-deployable within 30 to 120 seconds. Detonation of its built-in charges clears both landmines and barbed wire from a pathway 3 feet wide and 146 feet long.[10]

Another demining techique, mechanical clearance, involves the use of specialized vehicles such as mine rollers, mine flails, and mine plows. Mine rollers, also known as mine trawls, were introduced in World War I. Attached to the front of armored vehicles, these devices are designed to detonate mines as they cross a battlefield, clearing a path for troops and other vehicles to follow. Mine flails, invented during World War II, flog the soil with heavy chains or cables. Both systems are still in use, but they often leave unexploded mines behind. Some studies suggest that mine flails miss 40 to 50 percent of the mines in

(continues)

A soldier of 162 Engineer Company Army National Guard attached with 2nd Combat Engineer Battalion of U.S. Marine Corps prepares a mine roller for a mission in southern Afghanistan in March 2010. *(Shamil Zhumatov/Reuters/Corbis)*

(continued)

a given location.[11] Mine plows, attached to tanks or modified bulldozers, expose mines while leaving the task of deactivation to EOD experts.

Most modern humanitarian demining relies on manual detection and disarmament. A somewhat safer method is remote burning, which requires EOD technicians to cut holes in a mine and douse it with diethylenetriamine, a chemical that reacts with various TNT-based explosives to create spontaneous combustion, burning off a mine's explosive charge without detonation. Diethylenetriamine does not, however, react with the explosive RDX or others based on pentaerythritol tetranitrate (PETN), leaving humans the slow and dangerous task of dismantling these individual charges.[12]

(Continued from page 83)

to discuss RSP techniques, for fear of helping would-be bombers build better, more dangerous IEDs, but certain broad methods are recognized. They include:

- *Controlled explosions.* Suspected IEDs may be destroyed in lieu of attempting to disarm them, either by gunfire or by application of a small explosive charge designed to shatter the bomb's trigger mechanism without detonating the main charge. Relatively small packages are frequently removed from their original position to a safer place for destruction; suspected car bombs may be isolated by police cordons and roadblocks. Robots are often used to transport a suspected IED and to destroy it without risking human life. In some cases, like the car destroyed at Britain's Royal Alexandra Hospital in July 2007, the IED report proves to be a false alarm.[14]
- *Disruption.* This method of disarming bombs without exploding them involves high-pressure streams of water fired at the suspected IED, often by robots equipped with water cannons, while human

operators remain at a safe distance. Ideally, the water jet will drown, short-circuit, or break up an IED's electric components without causing the main charge to explode. British EOD technicians pio-

A soldier experiments with a Cutlass Bomb Disposal robot, a new vehicle to be used for bomb disposal and antiterrorism operations worldwide. *(Associated Press)*

neered disruption in 1972 with a device called the "Pigstick," which was mounted on a Wheelbarrow hazardous-duty robot. Now used worldwide, or copied by competing manufacturers, the Pigstick is also sometimes called a percussion activated neutralizer (PAN). By any name, it saves innocent lives.

o *Manual deactivation.* The last resort of any bomb-disposal expert is the hands-on approach, which carries the greatest risk of death or crippling injury. Seen more often in fiction and film than in real life, such risky methods are still required on occasion, such as when IEDs or other charges are found in locations where robots are useless and other techniques are ruled out for whatever reason. Manual deactivation (or defusing) requires one or more experts to penetrate a bomb's outer shell or container and disarm its trigger mechanism or timing device while at the same time remaining alert for any built-in anti-handling devices. Special tools for manual deactivation include drills that project fluid onto or into the bomb, and implements made from plastic or ceramics to avoid electric sparks. Most bomb-disposal experts killed on duty lose their lives during manual deactivation of IEDs or UXO.

DRESSING TO SURVIVE

Whenever bombs must be approached or handled, those assigned to deal with them wear special clothing designed to help them survive an explosion with minimal injury. No gear devised so far can guarantee survival, but with rare exceptions bomb disposal experts use any protective clothing available.

The basic concept of body armor has not changed much since ancient times, when suits of iron and steel were worn to deflect spears and arrows, or swords at close quarters. Body armor serves two basic functions: first, to stop weapons or projectiles from penetrating the wearer's body; and second, to diffuse violent impact and thus minimize blunt-trauma injury.

The National Institute of Justice recognizes seven classes of modern body armor, which are based on resistance to specific calibers of firearms.[15] In general, however, bomb-disposal officers are less concerned with being shot (though shrapnel penetration is a threat)

A bomb-disposal expert in a protective suit extracts a suspicious-looking package left near a populated area. *(AFP/Getty Images)*

"IRON MIKE"

Master Sergeant Michael Burghardt joined the United States Marine Corps in 1987, when he was just 18 years old. Three years later, he completed training as an EOD technician, qualified to disarm all types of military warheads and IEDs. By 2005, when he received a Bronze Star for disarming 64 terrorist bombs and 1,548 pieces of military ordnance in Iraq, he was known to his fellow Marines as "Iron Mike."[16]

On September 19, 2005, MSgt. Burghardt nearly died. He was summoned to a bomb site in Ramadi, where a blast had killed four American soldiers, leaving a crater eight feet wide and five feet deep. Troops at the scene knew that terrorists often plant multiple bombs in the same location, hoping to claim more victims when rescuers rush to the aid of their wounded comrades.

Burghardt approached the crater without first donning his bulky bomb-protection suit. As he later explained to reporters, "You can't react to any sniper fire and you get tunnel-vision."[17] Protected only by a helmet and flak vest, Burghardt found and disarmed two more IEDs, then located a third—beneath his feet.

Shifting soil warned Burghardt of the danger. Glancing down, he saw the base station of a Senao long-range cordless telephone trailing a length of wire, which he cut with a knife. Then, he says, "I found a piece of red detonating cord between my legs. That's when I knew I was screwed."[18]

As Burghardt shouted a warning to soldiers nearby, an unseen bomber keyed his own cell phone to detonate the IED.

than with explosive impact and potential burns. Blast-resistant suits are made from tightly woven synthetic aramid (aromatic polyamide) fibers, introduced by the DuPont chemical company in the early 1960s. The most common commercial name-brand of aramid fiber is Kevlar, which is used in most "bulletproof" vests. Aramid fibers are also flame-

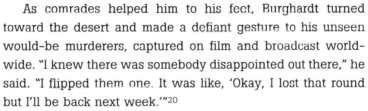

"A chill went up the back of my neck," Burghardt recalled, "and then the bomb exploded. As I was in the air I remember thinking, 'I don't believe they got me.' I was just ticked off they were able to do it. Then I was lying on the road, not able to feel anything from the waist down. My dad's a Vietnam vet who's paralyzed from the waist down. I was lying there thinking I didn't want to be in a wheelchair next to my dad and for him to see me like that. They started to cut away my pants and I felt a real sharp pain and blood trickling down. Then I wiggled my toes and I thought, 'Good, I'm in business.'"[19]

As comrades helped him to his feet, Burghardt turned toward the desert and made a defiant gesture to his unseen would-be murderers, captured on film and broadcast worldwide. "I knew there was somebody disappointed out there," he said. "I flipped them one. It was like, 'Okay, I lost that round but I'll be back next week.'"[20]

And so he was, continuing the war against terrorist fanatics. "It's a big game of chess," Burghardt says. "They're thinking their steps through on how to beat us, and we're doing the same thing. It's almost like a drug habit. There are the guys on the top who have the money and do the planning, and then there are the crack addicts down below. They make their living planting IED after IED until somebody puts a bullet in them."[21]

With IEDs blamed for half of all American combat deaths in Iraq, plus an ever-rising number of civilian victims—79 in the first three weeks of January 2009 alone—EOD specialists like MSgt. Burghardt are badly needed.[22]

resistant, and "bomb suits" normally have interior pockets for steel or ceramic ballistic plates to prevent penetration by shrapnel.[23]

While a full-body, blast-resistant suit protects the wearer's torso and limbs, other components complete the wardrobe. Helmets are standard, generally with an aramid core surrounded by a rigid outer layer and a transparent visor made from anti-ballistic plastic. Many have built-in headphones and microphones for communication, a self-contained ventilation system that cools the technician's head and keeps the visor from fogging, and an exterior mount for a hands-free light and/or video camera. High collars typically shield the officer's neck and allow for free movement of the head. Aramid boots protect the feet, and most bomb suits include quick-release latches or straps in case the operator requires emergency medical treatment.

One thing often missing from bomb suits is a pair of gloves. Special gloves (or gauntlets) do exist and are useful when a technician has to transport bombs by hand, but the thick material reduces manual dexterity required for dismantling intricate, sensitive IEDs or UXO. Most technicians, therefore, work bare-handed when disarming bombs, which accounts for frequent loss of hands or fingers during accidental detonations.

A new and still experimental form of "liquid body armor" employs special shear-thickening fluid (STF)—which hardens to a solid within milliseconds after suffering traumatic impact—sandwiched between layers of woven or solid material. No such bomb suits have been deployed in the field, but many bomb suits and bulletproof vests are saturated in fluid consisting of silica particles and polyethylene glycol diluted with ethanol; these vests are then baked in ovens to evaporate the ethanol. The resultant fabric is as flexible as ordinary aramid, but violent impact causes the STF to harden rapidly. Four layers of STF-treated aramid can disperse the same amount of energy as 14 layers of untreated Kevlar—and the fabric soon regains its normal flexibility.[24]

Loose Nukes

Pelindaba Nuclear Facility, South Africa

Shortly after midnight on November 8, 2007, four armed men invaded the Pelindaba Nuclear Facility in South Africa, located 18 miles west of Pretoria. According to the South African Nuclear Energy Corporation, a government body that runs the Pelindaba site, the "technically sophisticated criminals" deactivated multiple layers of security, including a 10,000-volt electric fence, to penetrate the site where large amounts of weapons-grade uranium are stored.[1] Closed-circuit television cameras tracked their progress, but it made no difference because Pelindaba's guards had left the monitors unattended.

Once inside, the intruders spent 45 minutes prowling around Pelindaba, which is ranked as one of South Africa's most heavily guarded "national key points," defined by government standards as "any place or area that is so important that its loss, damage, disruption or immobilization may prejudice the Republic."[2] They broke into the site's emergency control center and stole a computer, then breached an electronically sealed control room before security officer Anton Gerber surprised them. Shot and wounded in the struggle, Gerber triggered an alarm that set off lights and sirens, forcing the invaders to drop their stolen computer and flee. They evaded police from a nearby barracks, and while officers announced the arrest of three unnamed suspects on November 16, official statements in December 2008 claiming that no one was detained contradicted that report.[3]

The Pelindaba break-in, described as suggesting inside knowledge of the plant on the part of the perpetrators, resulted in dismissal of three guards. The invasion seemed all the more shocking because Pelindaba's security had been tightened after a lone intruder breached its defenses in 2006. The sole consolation was that no nuclear material was stolen—this time.

THE NUCLEAR AGE

Nuclear weapons are those that derive their destructive power either from fission or a combination of fission and fusion. None of these weapons existed prior to World War II, when the United States built the first "atomic bombs" and detonated two over Japan in August 1945, killing at least 120,000 people in the initial blasts and leaving 284,000 more to die from radiation poisoning or related diseases over the next half-century.[4]

No nuclear weapons have been used in warfare since 1945, although tests and demonstrations of various bigger and "better" nukes produced 2,045 more detonations between 1945 and 1996.[5] Physicists Edward Teller and Stanisław Ulam invented the hydgrogen bomb in 1951, leading to its first test detonation on the Pacific atoll of Eniwetok a year later. The next major development—conceived by Samuel Cohen at California's Lawrence Livermore National Laboratory in 1958 and tested in Nevada during 1963—was the neutron bomb, also called an enhanced radiation (ER) weapon. ER bombs and warheads are designed primarily to kill biological targets (humans, animals, and plants) through exposure to deadly radiation without inflicting catastrophic damage on buildings. A final type of nuclear weapon—"salted" warheads—surround the standard warhead with a "blanket" of materials, including cobalt, gold, tantalum, or zinc, designed to contaminate target areas with radiation for periods ranging from four months to five years after detonation.[6]

As of 2010, nine nations—the United States, Great Britain, Russia, France, China, India, Pakistan, Israel, and North Korea—are known to hold stockpiles of nuclear weapons. South Africa constructed at least six nuclear weapons during the 1970s and 1980s, but reportedly dismantled them before the end of the 20th century. Speculation persists about efforts to build nuclear weapons in other countries, including

Libya, Syria (where Israeli warplanes bombed a supposed shipment of North Korean nuclear material in 2007), and Iran (according to claims from President George W. Bush's administration in 2003–08).

On May 5, 2009, North Korea conducted a nuclear test explosion—said to be its second, though the first (in October 2006) was never positively verified—and the country is now recognized as a "fully fledged nuclear power" by spokesmen for the International Atomic Energy Agency. On February 9, 2010, Iranian leaders announced their country's successful production of enriched uranium—used in medical equipment, nuclear power stations, and weapons—but still publicly denied any intent to build nuclear bombs "unless we need to."

CONTROLLING NUKES

In July 1957 the International Atomic Energy Agency was created, with headquarters in Austria, to promote peaceful uses of nuclear power worldwide and limit the spread of nuclear weapons. Various treaties signed by major nations since the mid-1960s banned test detonations above ground, underwater, or in outer space (1963); banned placement of nuclear weapons in space (1967); prevented the spread of nuclear weapons to further nations (1968); limited the number of anti-ballistic missiles built in Russia and America (1972); restricted growth of offensive weapons systems and strategic systems (1979); banned intermediate-range and short-range missiles (1987); reduced the standing number of warheads and delivery vehicles held by the United States and Russia (1991 and 1993); and banned further nuclear testing by signatory nations (1996). However, since only 94 countries signed the final treaty, development and testing of new weapons subsequently occurred in India and Pakistan.[7]

In 1996 the United Nations International Court of Justice (ICJ) issued an advisory opinion on the "Legality of the Threat or Use of Nuclear Weapons," declaring that "the threat or use of nuclear weapons would generally be contrary to the rules of international law applicable in armed conflict, and in particular the principles and rules of humanitarian law; however, in view of the current state of international law, and of the elements of fact at its disposal, the Court

(Continues on page 98)

ABDUL QADEER KHAN

Born in India to Muslim parents, Abdul Khan was 11 years old when British colonial forces granted independence to his homeland in August 1947. At the same time, Pakistan was born from two corners of India, removing 31 million Muslims from rule by India's Hindu majority.[8] Khan's family waited another five years to leave India for Pakistan, where Khan obtained a degree in metallurgy from the University of Karachi in 1960. He later moved to Holland and earned an engineering degree in 1967, and then went on to Belgium to receive a Ph.D. in metallurgy five years later. He was working with enriched uranium in Holland when India detonated its first nuclear weapon in May 1974 and Pakistani scientists began scrambling to build their own.

In December 1975 Khan stole secret blueprints for the Dutch gas centrifuge, used to manufacture nuclear weapons, and smuggled them into Pakistan. Prime Minister Zulfikar Ali Bhutto placed Khan in charge of Pakistan's uranium enrichment program, working at a lab in Kahuta, Rawalpindi, which now bears his name. In 1983 a Dutch court tried Khan *in absentia* for attempted espionage and sentenced him to a four-year prison term. In 1987 Khan announced that Pakistan had completed work on its first nuclear weapons and denied any reliance on foreign technology. "All the research work," he said, "was the result of our innovation and struggle. We did not receive any technical know-how from abroad, but we can't reject the use of books, magazines, and research papers in this connection."[9]

In May 1998 *Newsweek* magazine accused Khan of offering nuclear knowledge for sale to Iraq's Saddam Hussein. Khan denied it, but rival bomb tests conducted a few days later confirmed beyond doubt that both India and Pakistan possessed nuclear weapons. Meanwhile, American authorities charged that Pakistan was trading nuclear weapons technology with

North Korea in return for ballistic missile technology required to deliver Pakistani warheads. With U.S. military and financial aid to Pakistan cut off, Pakistan President Pervez Musharraf announced Khan's dismissal from his lab command in March 2001. It was not punishment, however, as Khan moved into a ministerial position as Special Science and Technology Adviser to the President.

Scrutiny of Khan increased after the terrorist attacks of September 11, 2001. American forces retaliated by invading Afghanistan, Pakistan's next-door neighbor, and routing the extremist Taliban government that had sheltered the al-Qaeda members who planned the attacks. Washington claimed that al-Qaeda had tried to buy nuclear materials from Pakistan, and in October 2001 Pakistani authorities jailed three scientists from the lab once run by Khan.

In 2003, after U.S. troops invaded Iraq to seize weapons of mass destruction that never surfaced, Washington accused Khan of selling nuclear material and centrifuges to Libyan President Muammar al-Gaddafi. In December 2003, around the same time Pakistani police jailed two more scientists from Khan's old lab on suspicion of selling nuclear technology to Iran, Libya announced the scrapping of its nuclear weapons program. On January 31, 2004, President Musharraf dismissed Khan from his government post. Four days later Khan appeared on television and confessed to running an international ring that sold nuclear technology to anti-American nations, including Iran, Libya, and North Korea. Though he was not charged with any crime, Khan received a pardon from President Musharraf on February 5 and was placed under house arrest in Karachi.

Under pressure in confinement, Khan's health began to fail. Pakistani authorities denied reports of a heart attack in February 2004, but they announced his diagnosis of cancer in

(continues)

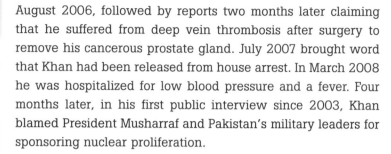

(continued)

August 2006, followed by reports two months later claiming that he suffered from deep vein thrombosis after surgery to remove his cancerous prostate gland. July 2007 brought word that Khan had been released from house arrest. In March 2008 he was hospitalized for low blood pressure and a fever. Four months later, in his first public interview since 2003, Khan blamed President Musharraf and Pakistan's military leaders for sponsoring nuclear proliferation.

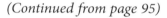

(Continued from page 95)

cannot conclude definitively whether the threat or use of nuclear weapons would be lawful or unlawful in an extreme circumstance of self-defence, in which the very survival of a State would be at stake."[10] In short, the ruling solved nothing, and it could not bind nations that reject the ICJ's authority.

The threat of nuclear terrorism increased after 1991, when the Soviet Union was dissolved into 15 independent, and sometimes hostile, nations. Under communism, nuclear facilities had been erected in many of those countries; these facilities are now abandoned, with weapons-grade radioactive material left behind. A report issued by Harvard University in 2005 announced that former Soviet republics contained enough material to build 80,000 nuclear weapons, and that only half of it was properly secured.[11] In January 2006 the International Atomic Energy Agency reported more than 100 incidents of nuclear smuggling in the past 13 years, but denied that any completed Soviet bombs or warheads were missing.[12] Aleksey Yabokov, an adviser to Russian ex-president Boris Yeltsin, disagrees. In 1997 he told Congress that Russia had built 80 to 100 suitcase-sized nuclear weapons, each equivalent to 1,000 tons of TNT in destructive power, and that *all* of them were missing.[13]

NEST

Nuclear blackmail is a frequent subject of spy novels and films, starting with *The 49th Man* in 1953. The most famous fictional tale is probably *Thunderball*, a James Bond adventure published by author Ian Fleming in 1961, adapted for the big screen in 1965, and remade in 1983 as *Never Say Never Again*. In that story, criminals hijack a Royal Air Force Bomber and steal two nuclear weapons, demanding a ransom of £100,000,000 ($142,243,000) to avert destruction of Miami, Florida.

Sadly, such crimes are not confined to fiction. In 1974 extortionists threatened to destroy Boston, Massachusetts, with a nuclear bomb unless they received a $200,000 payoff. FBI agents and members of the Atomic Energy Commission (AEC) rushed to Boston with radiation-detection equipment, but they had no idea where to look for the bomb. Agents delivered the ransom as ordered, but no one arrived to collect it. The incident was finally dismissed as a hoax. The individuals behind it remain unidentified today.[14]

Between April 1970 and November 1974, at least 45 troublesome incidents involving nuclear power plants or materials were recorded. Thirty-eight of those cases involved bomb threats to nuclear facilities in the United States, where an IED explosion might conceivably produce a disaster equal to Russia's Chernobyl meltdown of April 1986. No warning preceded the detonation of a firebomb at the Pilgrim nuclear facility near Plymouth, Massachusetts, in August 1974. Unknown prowlers tried to breach a fence at a facility in Oak Ridge, Tennessee, two months later, and Italian police foiled an extremist plot to poison city water supplies with radioactive material that same year. Most disturbing were three incidents involving loss or theft of nuclear materials in the United States.[15]

In 1975, responding to the hoax threat against Boston, President Gerald Ford created the Nuclear Emergency Search Team (NEST)—later renamed the Nuclear Emergency Support Team—within the Department of Energy's National Nuclear Security Administration. NEST consists of some 1,100 nuclear physicists, chemists, engineers, meteorologists (weather experts), doctors, nurses, computer specialists, and security experts employed at various nuclear facilities around

(Continued on page 102)

DIRTY BOMBS

"Dirty bombs" are technically known as *radiological dispersal devices* (RDDs). They are designed to contaminate the area of detonation with high levels of dangerous radioactivity. In theory, RDDs may be fabricated by packing radioactive material around an IED made with conventional explosives. According to the Council on Foreign Relations, Iraq tested a one-ton radiological bomb in 1987, and then dropped the program when its yield proved insufficient to cause widespread death or illness. Eight years later, Chechen rebels planted a dirty bomb made from dynamite and cesium 137 in Moscow's Izmaylovsky Park, but it failed to detonate. A second, similar bomb was found and disarmed in Argun, 10 miles east of the Chechen capital at Grozny, during December 1998.[16]

On May 8, 2002, federal agents in Chicago charged U.S. citizen José Padilla (alias Abdullah al-Muhajir or Muhajir Abdullah) as a material witness in an alleged conspiracy to build and detonate a dirty bomb on American soil. (No such bomb was ever found.) A month later, on June 9, President George W. Bush declared Padilla an "enemy combatant" who was not entitled to a trial or any other rights guaranteed to American citizens under the U.S. Constitution. Padilla spent the next 42 months in military custody, until public protest forced the government to file legal charges in January 2006. Padilla faced trial in Miami, where jurors convicted him of conspiracy in August 2007. Judge Marcia Cooke sentenced Padilla to a 17-year prison term in January 2008. While his case is on appeal, he remains confined at a federal "supermax" prison in Colorado.

In August 2004 British authorities arrested another alleged dirty-bomb conspirator, Dhiren Barot, who was born in India and immigrated to England with his family at age two, in 1973. Barot converted to Islam in 1991 and traveled to Pakistan four years later, joining in attacks on Indian troops in Kashmir. Police say that he joined al-Qaeda sometime before he returned to Britain, in April 2001. His arrest resulted from the 2004 seizure of a laptop computer and 51 compact discs in Pakistan listing terrorist tactics and targets marked for destruction in Great Britain and the United States. Jailed with seven other British residents of Pakistani descent, Barot faced charges of conspiracy to commit murder; conspiracy to commit a public nuisance using radioactive material, toxic gases, and explosives; and possession of detailed surveillance reports on targets, including the International Monetary Fund and World Bank buildings in Washington, D.C., the New York Stock Exchange, various Citigroup buildings, and Prudential Financial buildings in Newark, New Jersey.

According to investigators, Barot and his friends planned to use dirty bombs that would detonate in limousines stationed outside their various targets. Prosecutors admitted that the plotters had no money and had never purchased any vehicles or explosives, but they proceeded to trial on conspiracy charges (which simply involve a criminal plan). In November 2006 Barot pled guilty on one charge (conspiracy to commit murder) and received a life sentence with recommendation that he serve at least 40 years. An appellate court reduced his sentence to 30 years, ruling that his plot had not been "viable."[17]

Despite the fact that only two RDDs have been documented, and both of them failed to explode, widespread fear surrounds the notion of terrorists planting dirty bombs in major cities. "Terror warnings" from the U.S. Department of Homeland Security stoke such fears, but various researchers say that homemade dirty bombs are unlikely to cause many more fatalities than a large conventional IED. The U.S. Department of Energy says that civilian contamination would be "fairly high," but rarely fatal, if no effort was made to clean up in the aftermath of a dirty bomb explosion. Public fear might cause chaos, and economic losses would be suffered during a protracted cleanup, but researchers have compared a homemade RDD's personal impact to smoking five packs of cigarettes or eating ice cream on a daily basis.[18]

(Continued from page 99)

the United States. They are specially trained and equipped to locate warheads or homemade weapons of mass destruction. While few are trained in combat, they have shared their expertise with members of the U.S. Army's Delta Force, the U.S. Navy's SEALS, and other elite military units likely to be called upon in a real-life hunt for nuclear weapons and extortionists. Government spokesmen maintain that NEST units can reach any point in the United States within four hours of receiving an alert, but some wonder if that is good enough.[19]

By December 2000, NEST had responded to 125 alarms, 95 of which were deemed hoaxes.[20] Some of those cases include the following:

- *January 1975*: Alleged members of the Weather Underground claimed nuclear bombs had been placed in three Los Angeles build-

Members of the Louisiana Army National Guard's 62nd Weapons of Mass Destruction–Civil Support Team are debriefed after a "dirty bomb" exercise. *(Associated Press)*

ings. While the threat included a drawing of a functional warhead, NEST found no bombs.

o *November 1976*: Unknown extortionists threatened to detonate 10 "dirty bombs" in Spokane, Washington, if they were not paid $500,000. Again, no bombs were found.

o *January 1979*: A bitter ex-employee of a nuclear plant in North Carolina left radioactive material at the plant manager's home, with a note demanding $100,000 to avoid dispersal of hazardous waste throughout the city. The extortionist was convicted and imprisoned.

o *April 1979*: California Governor Jerry Brown received a postcard warning that plutonium had been released in the state capitol building to "demonstrate the folly of nuclear energy." NEST found nothing.[21]

o *November 1987*: An alleged Cuban activist warned police in Indianapolis that a nuclear device was planted in a local bank. NEST found no weapon.

o *April 1990*: NEST responded to threats of an impending nuclear explosion in El Paso, Texas, but located no weapon or radioactive material.

o *February 1999*: An unknown caller warned FBI agents that nuclear material was hidden on a train traveling from Chicago to Seattle. NEST stopped and searched the train in Montana, but found nothing.

A NEST response to nuclear threats proceeds according to established stages. First, intelligence must be collected, normally from agents of the FBI or Central Intelligence Agency (CIA), who may receive warnings from local authorities. Next, NEST goes on standby alert, rallying an Operational Emergency Management Team. That unit performs a credibility assessment, deciding whether the threat is an obvious hoax or poses some plausible danger. If the threat is deemed credible, NEST proceeds to a search, employing various state-of-the-art radiation-detection devices. No NEST deployment has yet proceeded beyond that point, but if a weapon is found, the searchers proceed to recovery and ordnance disposal. In the event of a catastrophe, NEST also participates in consequence management, collaborating with local physicians and members of the Federal Emergency Management Agency to minimize damage and panic.[22]

Despite NEST's record of debunking nuclear threats, the alarms continue. Between September 12, 2001, and August 26, 2002, NEST investigated 70 incidents of "communicated nuclear threats and reports of illicit trafficking of nuclear materials" nationwide, without discovering an actual weapon or cache of radioactive matter.[23] Considering the fact that terrorists may strike without warning, NEST also performs random sweeps of Washington, D.C., and other major U.S. cities, even when no threats have been received. If and when an active nuclear device is found on American soil, responsibility for disarming it will fall to special EOD units maintained on perpetual alert by the U.S. Army, Navy, Air Force, and Marine Corps.

Chronology

9th century	Chinese alchemists discover gunpowder while seeking immortality
1605	**March :** Guy Fawkes's Gunpowder Plot against Parliament in London goes awry
1846	Italian chemist Ascanio Sobrero discovers nitroglycerine
1863	German chemist Joseph Wilbrand invents TNT
1866	Swedish chemist Alfred Nobel invents dynamite
1875	Alfred Nobel invents gelignite, the first plastic explosive
1883	**March :** London's Metropolitan Police create a Special Irish Branch to curb terrorist bombings
1886	**May 4:** Bombs and gunfire kill eight policemen and four civilians in Chicago's Haymarket Square
1903	**April:** NYPD created an Italian Squad to curb Black Hand bombings
1905	**December 30:** A terrorist bomb kills former governor Frank Steunenberg at his home in Caldwell, Idaho
1914	**August 1:** NYPD creates its bomb squad
1916	**July 22:** A bomb kills 10 victims and wounds 40 during San Francisco's Preparedness Day parade
1917	**November 24:** A bomb kills seven officers at Milwaukee police headquarters
1919	**April 30:** New York City postal workers find 16 mail bombs addressed to prominent persons

	June 2: Eight anarchist bombs explode in Washington, D.C., and four other cities, killing two bombers, a policeman, and a civilian bystander
1920	**September 16:** A bombing on New York's Wall Street kills 38 victims and injures 400
1927	**May 18:** Deranged tax protester Andrew Kehoe bombs a school in Bath Township, Michigan, killing himself and 45 others, and injuring 58
1928	**April:** Gangsters detonate 61 bombs during Chicago's "Pineapple Primary" election
1940	**July 4:** NYPD bomb squad officers Joseph Lynch and Ferdinand Socha die while trying to defuse a bomb at the World's Fair
1947	**August 18:** Klansmen in Birmingham, Alabama, detonate the first of 41 bombs spanning 16 years
1955	**November 1:** Jack Graham bombs United Airlines Flight 629 in Colorado, killing 44, to collect life insurance on his mother
1957	**November 11:** New York police arrest "Mad Bomber" George Metesky, who has planted 33 bombs and wounded 15 victims since 1940
1958	**October 12:** Neo-Nazis bomb the Hebrew Benevolent Congregation Temple in Atlanta, Georgia
1959	**September 15:** A suicide bomber kills himself and five others and wounds 19 at Houston's Edgar Allan Poe Elementary School
1960	**October:** New York City's unidentified "Sunday Bomber" kills one and wounds 51 with bombs planted on ferries and subways
1961	**August 28:** Puerto Rico Police Officer Angel Cordero-Roman dies while defusing a bomb in San Juan
1963	**September 15:** Klansmen bomb Birmingham's Sixteenth Street Baptist Church, killing four girls
1969	**October 14:** An explosion at Macy's department store injures two NYPD Bomb Squad officers

1970	**October 15:** Congress passes the Federal Explosives Control Statute
1971	**September 9:** Capt. David Stewardson dies while defusing a bomb in Belfast, Northern Ireland
1972	**March 15:** Staff Sgt. Christopher Cracknell and Staff Sgt. Anthony Butcher die while defusing a bomb in Belfast
	July 1: The Bureau of Alcohol, Tobacco and Firearms is created
	July 15: Capt. John Young dies while defusing a terrorist bomb in Silverbridge, Northern Ireland
1973	**September 23:** Capt. Ronald Wilkinson dies six days after defusing a bomb in Birmingham, England
	December 3: A bomb kills NYPD Bomb Squad Officer Vincent Connolly
1975	**January 31:** The Nuclear Emergency Search Team responds to its first threat in Los Angeles
1976	**March 2:** A deranged bomber kills himself, his wife, and three policemen at at a courthouse in Point Pleasant, West Virginia
	September 11: A bomb kills NYPD Bomb Squad Officer Brian Murray
1977	**January 9:** Sgt. Martin Walsh dies while defusing a bomb in Newtownbutler, Northern Ireland
1983	**October 23:** Bombers kill 241 U.S. Marines at their barracks in Beirut, Lebanon
	November 7: Members of the "Resistance Conspiracy" bomb the U.S. Senate
1985	**June 23:** A bomb destroys Air India Flight 182 off the Irish coast, killing 329
1986	**February 18:** A bomb kills LAPD Bomb Squad Detectives Ronald Ball and Arleigh McCree in Hollywood
1988	**December 21:** A Libyan bomb destroys Pan Am Flight 103 over Lockerbie, Scotland, killing 270

1992	**May 23:** Mafia bombers kill Magistrate Giovanni Falcone, his wife, and three bodyguards outside Palermo, Sicily
1993	**February 26:** A truck bomb kills six and wounds 1,042 at New York's World Trade Center
	March 12: Thirteen bombs explode in Bombay, India, killing 257 and wounding 713
1995	**April 19:** Timothy McVeigh bombs Oklahoma City's federal building, killing 168
1996	**April 3:** Authorities in Montana arrest "Unabomber" Theodore Kaczynski, who has killed three and wounded 21 with 16 bombs since May 1978
1998	**August 7:** Car bombs strike U.S. embassies in Dar es Salaam, Tanzania, and Nairobi, Kenya, killing 223 and wounding at least 4,085
2001	**September 11:** NYPD Bomb Squad Detective Danny Richards dies during rescue efforts following terrorist strikes at the World Trade Center
2002	**October 12:** A car bomb and a bomb detonated in a night club kill 202 in Bali, Indonesia
2004	**March 11:** Multiple bombings of commuter trains kill 191 and injure 2,050 in Madrid, Spain
2005	**July 7:** Suicide bombers kill 56 and wound over 700 on London subways
2007	**August 14:** Truck bombs in Kahtaniya, Iraq, kill 796
2008	**September 10:** British army ordinance expert Gary O'Donnell dies while defusing a bomb in Afghanistan

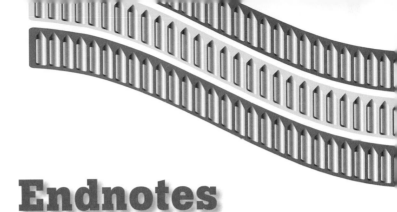

Endnotes

Introduction

1. Harlan Ullman and James Wade, *Shock and Awe: Achieving Rapid Dominance* (Washington, D.C.: National Defense University Press, 1996), xxiv.
2. The World of Explosives, "History of Explosives and Blasting," http://www.cxplosives.org/HistoryofExplosives.htm (Accessed December 11, 2009).
3. Ibid.
4. Bureau of Alcohol, Tobacco, Firearms, and Explosives, "U.S. Bomb Data Center Fact Sheet (September 2008)," http://www.atf.gov/publications/factsheets/factsheet-us-bomb-data-center.html (Accessed June 22, 2010).

Chapter 1

1. Jersey City Past and Present, "Black Tom Explosion," http://www.njcu.edu/programs/jchistory/Pages/B_Pages/ Black_Tom_Explosion.htm (Accessed December 11, 2009).
2. BrainyQuote, http://www.brainyquote.com/quotes/authors/s/scott_adams_2.html (Accessed June 4, 2010).
3. The World of Explosives, "How Explosives Work," http://www.explosives.org/How.htm (Accessed December 11, 2009).

4. The Associated Press, "Blasts and Fires Wreck Texas City of 15,000," *New York Times,* April 17, 1947; "Rumours linger over N Korea blast," BBC News, April 24, 2004; Oklahoma City National Memorial & Museum, http://www.oklahomacitynationalmemorial.org (Accessed December 11, 2009).
5. The World of Explosives, "How Explosives Work."
6. FBI, "Domestic Terrorism Program," http://baltimore.fbi.gov/domter.htm (Accessed December 11, 2009).
7. Michele Wilson and John Lynxwiler, "Abortion clinic violence as terrorism," *Studies in Conflict & Terrorism* 11 (1988): 263–273.
8. U.S. Army FM 20-32, *Mine/Countermine Operations* (Washington, D.C.: Department of the Army, 1998).

Chapter 2

1. Edward Mickolus, *Transnational Terrorism: A Chronology of Events, 1968–1979* (Westport, Conn.: Greenwood Press, 1980), 12–13.
2. Northern Ireland Society, http://cain.ulster.ac.uk/ni/security.htm#05 (Accessed December 11, 2009).
3. Christopher Dobson and Ronald Payne, *The Terrorists: Their*

Weapons, Leaders and Tactics (New York: Facts On File, 1982), 130–131.

4. Mickolus, 10–25; Arie Perliger and Leonard Weinberg, "Jewish self defense and terrorist groups prior to the establishment of the State of Israel: Roots and traditions," *Totalitarian Movements & Political Religions* 4 (2003): 100–101; J. Boyer Bell, *Terror Out of Zion* (New York: St. Martin's Press, 1977), 181.

5. Ron David, *Arabs & Israel for Beginners* (New York: Writers and Readers, 1996), 103.

6. Rep. Benjamin Gilman, "Middle Eastern Terrorist Incidents," *Congressional Record* (December 14, 2001): E2315-17.

7. "List of FALN Perpetrated Bombing and Incendiary Incidents," *Latin American Studies* (December 15, 1997), http://www.latinamericanstudies.org/puertorico/FALN-incidents.pdf (accessed December 11, 2009); Brent Smith, *Terrorism in America: Pipe Bombs and Pipe Dreams* (Albany, N.Y.: State University of New York Press, 1994), 22–23.

8. David Chalmers, *Hooded Americanism: The History of the Ku Klux Klan* (Durham, N.C.: Duke University Press, 1981), 197; Michael Newton, *The Ku Klux Klan* (Jefferson, N.C.: McFarland, 2007), 269.

9. Newton, 269–272, 384–386.

10. Ibid., 272–273, 388; Barbara Patterson, "Defiance and Dynamite," *New South* 18 (May 1963): 8–11.

11. Newton, 269.

12. John Douglas, Ann Burgess, Allen Burgess, and Robert Ressler, *Crime Classification Manual: A Standard System for Investigating and Classifying Violent Crimes* (San Francisco: Jossey-Bass, 1992), 186–187.

13. David Everitt, *Human Monsters: An Illustrated Encyclopedia of the World's Most Vicious Murderers* (Chicago: Contemporary Books, 1993), 96–99.

14. TruTV, "Ted Kaczynski: The Unabomber," http://www.trutv.com/library/crime/terrorists_spies/terrorists/kaczynski/1.html (Accessed May 19, 2010).

15. "15 Were Injured by Bomb Blasts," *New York Times,* January 23, 1957.

16. James Brussel, *Casebook of a Crime Psychiatrist* (New York: Bernard Geis Associates, 1968), 7–73.

17. Ibid.

18. Kristen Wyatt, "Eric Rudolph, Proud Killer," *Decatur Daily* (Alabama), April 14, 2005.

19. Nick Hopkins and Sarah Hall, "David Copeland: a Quiet Introvert, Obsessed with Hitler and Bombs," *The Guardian* (London), June 30, 2000.

20. Michael Newton, *The Encyclopedia of Unsolved Crimes* (New York: Facts On File, 2004), 246–48, 299–302.

21. Department of Homeland Security, Office for Bombing Prevention, http://www.dhs.gov/xabout/structure/gc_1184010933025.shtm (Accessed May 29, 2010).

22. Ibid.

Chapter 3

1. Tatiana Hensley, "Bolles: Cautious man, dedicated journalist," *Arizona Republic,* May 28, 2006.

2. "A Chronology of the Major Events in the Car-Bomb Murder of *Arizona Republic* Reporter Don Bolles," *Arizona Republic,* June 3, 2001.

3. U.S. Code art. 18, part I, chap. 96 §§ 1961–1968.

4. Thomas Pitkin and Francesco Cordasco, *The Black Hand: A Chapter in Ethnic Crime* (Totowa, N.J.: Littlefield, Adams, & Co., 1977).

5. "Think Prisoners Are Union Strike Bombers," *New York Times,* May 21, 1921.

6. James Merriner, "Political hits," *Illinois Issues* 26 (September 2000), 22–23.

7. Urban Dictionary, "Youngstown Tuneup," http://www.urban-dictionary.com/define.php?term=youngstown%20 tuneup (Accessed December 11, 2009); Don Stradley, "Pavlik giving media a reason not to dwell on Youngstown's past," ESPN (October 16, 2008), http://m.espn.go.com/general/boxing/story?storyId=3645706 (Accessed December 11, 2009).

8. T.J. English, *Paddy Whacked* (New York: Regan Books, 2005), 368–377.

9. John Dickie, *Cosa Nostra: A History of the Sicilian Mafia* (London: Coronet, 2004), 235.

10. Richard Esposito and Ted Gerstein, *Bomb Squad: A Year Inside the Nation's Most Exclusive Police Unit* (New York: Hyperion, 2007), 283–284.

11. Dickie, 379–403.

12. Dickie, 407–443; "Mafia bosses convicted in bombing," CBC News, November 10, 2000; "Mafia 'gripping Italian economy,'" BBC News, November 14, 2000.

13. Grace Livingstone, *Inside Colombia: Drugs, Democracy, and War* (Piscataway, N.J.: Rutgers University Press, 2004), 55.

14. PBS, "Thirty Years of America's Drug War: a Chronology," http:// www.pbs.org/wgbh/pages/frontline/shows/drugs/cron (Accessed June 4, 2010).

15. U.S. State Department, "U.S. Agents Help Train Colombian Investigative Bomb Squads," http://www.globalsecurity.org/security/library/news/ 2005/06/sec-050602-usia02.htm (Accessed December 14, 2009).

16. Enric Volante, "Series of Blasts in '60s Seemed Part of Mob War—at Least, at First," *Arizona Daily Star,* February 1, 2004.

17. Enric Volante, "Admitted Bomber First Tipped Cops," *Arizona Daily Star,* February 2, 2004.

18. Enric Volante, "FBI Jumps, Then Shuts Down Probe," *Arizona Daily Star,* February 3, 2004.

19. Ward Churchill and Jim Vander Wall, *The COINTELPRO Papers: Documents from the FBI's Secret Wars Against Dissent in the United States* (Boston: South End Press, 1990), 41–45.

20. ATF Fact Sheet (January16, 2007), http://www.atf.gov/press/releases/2007/01/011607-doj-fact-sheet-on-gang-violence-efforts.html (Accessed June 22, 2010).

Chapter 4

1. "Send Death Bombs to 36 U.S. Leaders," *Chicago Tribune,* May 1, 1919.

2. Eiler Nyström (ed.), *Luxdorphs Dagbøger,* Vol. 1 (Copenhagen: Aarhundredes Stats, 1915), 207, 209.

3. "Police," *The Times* (London), July 20, 1889.

4. Chalmers, *Hooded Americanism,* 197; Mickolus, *Transnational Terrorism,* 11.

5. Mickolus, 21–26.

6. Jewish Virtual Library, "Alois Brunner," http://www.jewishvir-tuallibrary.org/jsource/Holocaust/Brunner.html (Accessed December 14, 2009).

7. Mickolus, 81–100, 430, 435, 437, 452, 455.

8. Mickolus, 239, 255, 292, 294, 333, 345–352, 354–355, 357, 361, 368, 371, 381.

9. Mickolus, 304, 403-405, 425, 435, 544, 851, 901–902, 904.

10. Mickolus, 403, 408, 455, 563, 591, 617, 677, 850.

11. NationMaster Encyclopedia, "Franz Fuchs," http://www.nationmaster.com/encyclopedia/Franz-Fuchs (Accessed December 14, 2009); "Middle Eastern Terrorist Incidents," *Congressional Record* (December 14, 2001): E2315–17.

12. Bite Back, http://directaction.info/news_dec28_08.htm (Accessed December 14, 2009).

13. "Letter-bombing caretaker jailed," BBC News, September 28, 2007.

Chapter 5

1. NationMaster Encyclopedia, "George Medal," http://www.nationmaster.com/encyclopedia/George-Medal (Accessed December 14, 2009).

2. "Bomb expert honoured for bravery," BBC News, February 13, 2007.

3. Ibid.

4. Ibid.

5. Jerome Starkey, "Bomb hero puts finger in trigger," *The Sun* (London), June 23, 2008.

6. Tom Dunn, "Taliban kill bomb squad legend Gary," *The Sun* (London), September 13, 2008.

7. ATF, "U.S. Bomb Data Center Fact Sheet (September 2008)," http://www.atf.gov/publications/factsheets/factsheet-us-bomb-data-center.html; Officer Down Memorial Page, http://www.odmp.org/browse.php (Accessed December 14, 2009).

8. William Adelman, *Haymarket Revisited* (Chicago: Illinois Labor History Society, 1986).

9. Officer Down Memorial Page Inc., http://www.odmp.org/browse.php (Accessed December 14, 2009).

10. Guerilla News Network, "Weather Underground Chronology," http://meme_mutation.gnn.tv/blogs/3900/Weather_Underground_Chronology (Accessed December 14, 2009).

11. Charles Jones, ed., *The Black Panther Party [Reconsidered]* (Baltimore: Black Classic Press, 1988), 426–27; Todd Cooper, "After 35 years, witness still says he was 911 caller. Duane Peak holds firm on the recording that led to the death of an Omaha officer and the convictions of two men in the 1970s," *Omaha World-Herald,* May 14, 2006.

12. Michael Smith, "Calls to honour inventor of bomb disposal device," *The Telegraph,* June 19, 2001.

13. Northrup Grumman, "Photo Release—Northrop Grumman Demonstrates CUTLASS Bomb Disposal Robot During UK Ministerial Visit (June 18, 2007)," http://www.irconnect.com/noc/press/pages/news_releases.html?d=121487 (Accessed December 14, 2009).

14. Nova, "Bomb Squad," http://www.pbs.org/wgbh/nova/robots (Accessed December 14, 2009).

15. Ibid.

16. Ibid.

17. Officer Down Memorial Page Inc., http://www.odmp.org/browse.php (Accessed December 14, 2009).

18. Ian McPhedran, "Mutts with a nose for dangerous duty," *Sydney Herald Sun*, January 3, 2009.

19. ATF, "U.S. Bomb Data Center Fact Sheet (September 2008)"; Officer Down Memorial Page Inc., http://www.odmp.org/browse.php (Accessed December 14, 2009).

20. Transportation Security Administration, "TSA Dogs & Aviation Security: Detection Canine Team," http://www.tsa.gov/lawenforcement/programs/editorial_multi_image_0003.shtm (Accessed August 10, 2010).

21. Sheila McLaughlin, "Police dogs get bulletproof vests," *Cincinnati Enquirer*, June 27, 2000; Eden Consulting Group, State Statutes (California), http://www.policek9.com/html/statutes.html (December 14, 2009); Federal Law Enforcement Protection Act of 2000, 114 Stat. 638, Public Law 106-254.

22. Eden Consulting Group, State Statutes (California).

23. Esposito, *Bomb Squad,* 277–278.

Chapter 6

1. "19th Century Bomb Found in Whale," BBC News, June 14, 2007.

2. Molly Bennett, "WSU Bomb Dog Balou Finds Explosives; Aids in Arrest," *The Signpost* (Weber State University), September 17, 2007.

3. Peter Turner and Caroleen Williams, "QR Hits a Homerun: Land-mine-Detection Systems Based on Quadrupole Resonance Technology Show Progress," *Journal of Mine Action* 9.2 (February 2006), http://maic.jmu.edu/JOURNAL/9.2/RD/williams/williams.htm (Accessed December 14, 2009).

4. United Nations Mine Action Service, *Remote Explosive Scent Tracing* (New York: United Nations, 2003), 1–17.

5. McPhedran, "Mutts with a Nose for Dangerous Duty."

6. Carl Kirchner Canine Consultants Inc., http://www.canineconsultants.com (Accessed December 14, 2009).

7. Jerry Bromenshenk, Colin Henderson, Robert Seccomb, Steven Rice, Robert Etter, Susan Bender, Philip Rodacy, Joseph Shaw, Nathan Seldomridge, Lee Spangler, and James Wilson, "Can Honey Bees Assist in Area Reduction and Landmine Detection?" Research, Development, and Technology in Mine Action, http://maic.jmu.edu/JOURNAL/7.3/focus/bromenshenk/bromenshenk.htm (Accessed December 14, 2009).

8. "US Military Trains 'Air Force' of Bomb-Sniffing Bees," Agence France-Presse, November 28, 2006; Lester Haines, "US Unleashes Bomb-Sniffing Bees," *The Register* (London), November 28, 2006; Deborah Baker, "Homeland Security Swarm," *Seattle Times,* December 9, 2006.

9. Zooillogix , "Can Bomb-Sniffing Bees Save Innocent Lives?," http://scienceblogs.com/zooillogix/2007/05/can_bomb sniffing_bees_save_inn.php (Accessed December 14, 2009).

10. "Here Come the Ratbots," BBC News, May 1, 2002; "Move Over Sniffer Dogs, Here Come Africa's Rats," Reuters, September 27, 2004.

11. "A Human-Animal-Robot Cooperative System for Anti-Personnel Mine Detection," http://intechweb. org/book.php?id=29 (Accessed June 22, 2010).

12. Jennette Townsend, "Pigs: A Demining Tool of the Future?" *Research, Technology and Development in Mine Action* (December 2003), http://maic.jmu.edu/Journal/7.3/focus/townsend2/townsend2.htm (Accessed December 14, 2009).

13. U.S. Navy Marine Mammal Mine Hunting Systems, http://www.spawar.navy.mil/sandiego/technology/mammals/mine_hunting.html (Accessed December 14, 2009).

14. T.L. King, F.M. Horine, K.C. Daly, and B.H. Smith, "Explosives Detection with Hard-Wired Moths," *IEEE Transactions on Instrumentation and Measurement* 53 (August 2004), 1113–1118; Glen Rains, Jeffrey Tomberlin, and Don Kulasuri, "Using Insect Sniffing Devices for Detection," *Trends in Biotechnology* 26 (June 2008), 288–294.

15. R.S. Burlage, M. Hunt, J. DiBenedetto, and M. Maston, "Bioreporter Bacteria for the Detection of Unexploded Ordnance," Demining Research at the University of Western Australia, http://www.mech.uwa.edu.au/jpt/demining/others/ornl/rsb.html (Accessed December 14, 2009).

16. National Transportation Safety Board, *Aircraft Accident Report: In-flight Breakup Over the Atlantic Ocean Trans World Airlines Flight 800 (Boeing 747-131, N93119, Near East Moriches, New York; July 17, 1996)*, http://www.ntsb.gov/Publictn/2000/AAR0003.pdf (Accessed December 14, 2009).

18. ACFNewSource, "Mine-sniffing Plants," http://www.acfnewsource.org/science/mine_sniffing_plants.html (Accessed December 14, 2009).

17. WhatReallyHappened.com, "Was TWA 800 Shot Down By a Military Missile?" http://whatreallyhappened.com/RANCHO/CRASH/TWA/twa.html (Accessed December 14, 2009); Hidden Mysteries, "Conspiracies and Coverups: TWA Flight 800 Disaster: Cover-up?," http://www.hiddenmysteries.org/conspiracy/conspiracy/twa800.html (Accessed December 14, 2009).

19. Steven Lee Myers, "Explosive Suggests Terrorists Downed Plane, Russia Says," *New York Times,* August 28, 2004.

20. Craig Whitlock, "Homemade, Cheap and Dangerous: Terror Cells Favor Simple Ingredients In Building Bombs," *Washington Post,* July 5, 2007.

21. Paul Mlakar Sr., W. Gene Corley, Mete Sozen, and Charles Thornton, "The Oklahoma City Bombing: Analysis of last damage to the Murrah Building," *Journal of Performance of Constructed Facilities* 12 (August 1998), 113–119.

22. John Kelly, "Omagh Bombing: Northern Ireland's Blackest Day," *Sky News,* February 27, 2008.

Chapter 7

1. EOD Heroes, http://www.eodhero.com (Accessed December 14, 2009).

2. InjuryBoard.com, "Unexploded Munitions at 16,000 U.S. Sites a Public Health Risk" (November 25, 2002), http://www.injuryboard.com/national-news/unexploded-munitions-at.aspx?googleid=27528 (Accessed December 14, 2009).

3. Kay Schriner, "Still Cleaning Up After 25 Years: Vietnam Focuses on Landmines, Unexploded Ordnance & Rehabilitation of War-related Disability," Disability World, http://www.disability-world.org/01-03_03/children/uxo.shtml (Accessed December 14, 2009).

4. U.S. Department of State, "Lega-cies of War: Unexploded Ord-nance in Laos," http://www.state.gov/p/eap/rls/rm/2010/04/140688.htm (Accessed June 22, 2010); UXO Lao, "Lao Unexploded Ord nance Programme," http://www.uxolao.org/uxo%20problem.html (Accessed June 22, 2010).

5. Anthony Shadid, "In Lebanon, a War's Lethal Harvest," *Washington Post,* September 26, 2006; Raed Rafei, "Lebanon: Unexploded ordnance still a hazard," *Los Angeles Times,* September 4, 2008.

6. Landmine & Cluster Munition Monitor, "Bosnia and Herzegov-ina," http://www.icbl.org/lm/2005/bosnia.html (Accessed December 14, 2009).

7. Joseph Needham, *Science and Civ-ilization in China* Vol. 5 (Taipei: Caves Books, 1986), 192.

8. Margaret Busé, "What You Should Know About Landmine Victims," *Focus on Victim and Survivor Assistance* 3 (Fall 1999), http://maic.jmu.edu/JOURNAL/3.3/focus/how_many_victims.htm (Accessed December 14, 2009).

9. International Campaign to Ban Landmines, "Convention on the Prohibition of the Use, Stockpil-ing, Production and Transfer of Anti-Personnel Mines and on Their Destruction," http://www.icbl.org/index.php/icbl/Treaties/MBT/Treaty-Text-in-Many-Languages/English (Accessed June 4, 2010).

10. U.S. Marine Corps, "Anti-Person-nel Obstacle Breaching System," http://www.usmc.mil/unit/pandr/Documents/Concepts/2000/PDFs/Chapter4/APOBS.PDF (Accessed June 4, 2010).

11. Geneva International Centre for Humanitarian Demining, *A Study of Mechanical Application in Dem-ining* (Geneva: GICHD, 2004), 10–23, 30–34.

12. National Mine Action Centers, "Mine Clearance Techniques and Technologies for Effective Human-itarian Demining," http://maic.jmu.edu/JOURNAL/6.1/features/habib/habib.htm (Accessed May 19, 2010).

13. Glossary of EOD Terminology, http://www.eoduk.com/services/glossary.php (Accessed August 10, 2010).

14. "How is a controlled explosion carried out?" BBC News, July 4, 2007.

15. National Institute of Justice, *Bal-listic Resistance of Personal Body Armor, NIJ Standard —0101.04*

(September 2000), http://www.ncjrs.gov/pdffiles1/nij/183651.pdf (Accessed December 14, 2009).

16. C. David Kotok, "Injured Marine defies attackers," *Omaha World-Herald,* September 24, 2005.

17. Ibid.

18. Ibid.

19. Ibid.

20. Ibid.

21. Monte Morin, "Marine bomb expert shaken but not deterred by IED," *Stars and Stripes,* January 15, 2006.

22. John Ward Anderson, Steve Fainaru, and Jonathan Finer, "Bigger, Stronger Homemade Bombs Now to Blame for Half of U.S. Deaths," *Washington Post,* October 26, 2005; Iraq Body Count, http://www.iraqbodycount.org/database/incidents/page1 (Accessed December 14, 2009).

23. How Stuff Works, "How Blast-resistant Clothing Works," http://science.howstuffworks.com/blast-resistant-clothing2.htm (Accessed December 14, 2009).

24. How Stuff Works, "How Liquid Body Armor Works," http://science.howstuffworks.com/liquid-body-armor1.htm (Accessed December 14, 2009).

Chapter 8

1. Micah Zenko, "A Nuclear Site Is Breached," *Washington Post,* December 20, 2007.

2. Ibid.

3. Zenko; I Luv South Africa, "Pelindaba Nuclear Breach Still a Mystery," (December 23, 2008), http://iluvsa.blogspot.com/2008/12/pelindaba-nuclear-breach-still-mystery.html (Accessed December 14, 2009).

4. "Hiroshima Marks 63rd Anniversary of A-bomb," *Asahi Shimbun,* August 7, 2008.

5. Stephen Schwartz, *Atomic Audit: The Costs and Consequences of U.S. Nuclear Weapons Since 1940* (Washington D.C.: Brookings Institution Press, 1998), 52.

6. Nuclear Weapon Archive, "Types of Nuclear Weapons," http://nuclearweaponarchive.org/Nwfaq/Nfaq1.html (Accessed December 14, 2009).

7. Nuclear Treaties & Agreements, http://library.thinkquest.org/17940/texts/timeline/treaties.html (Accessed June 23, 2010).

8. Samina Mahsud-Dornan, "Pakistan, Population Programmes and Progress," *Ulster Medical Journal* 76 (September 2007): 122–123.

9. KnowledgeRush, "Abdul Khan," http://www.knowledgerush.com/kr/encyclopedia/Abdul_Khan (Accessed December 14, 2009).

10. International Court of Justice, "Legality of the Threat or Use of Nuclear Weapons," http://www.icj-cij.org/docket/index.php?p1=3&p2=4&k=e1&case=95&code=unan&p3=4 (Accessed December 14, 2009).

11. "Hunting Loose Nukes in Eastern Europe," ABC News, October 13, 2005.

12. Council on Foreign Relations, "Loose Nukes," http://www.cfr.org/publication/9549/#3 (Accessed December 14, 2009).

13. Andrew Schneider, "Elite U.S. Team Works to Keep Nuclear Bombs from Terrorists," *St. Louis Post-Dispatch*, October 21, 2001.

14. Ibid.

15. Mickolus, *Transnational Terrorism,* 171, 231, 248, 278, 304, 312, 325, 329–330, 334, 349, 351, 354, 357, 363, 373, 381, 395, 401, 417, 428, 430, 441, 452, 457, 465, 470–475, 486–487.

16. Council on Foreign Relations, "Dirty Bombs," http://www.cfr. org/publication/9548/#3 (Accessed December 14, 2009).

17. "'Dirty Bomb' Man's Sentence Cut," BBC News, May 16, 2007.

18. V.P. Reshetin, "Estimation of Radioactivity Levels Associated with a 90Sr Dirty Bomb Event," *Atmospheric Environment* 39 (2005): 4471–4477; J.P. Ring, "Radiation Risks and Dirty Bombs," *Radiation Safety Journal, Supplement 1* 86 (2004): S42–47.

19. Schneider, "Elite U.S. Team Works to Keep Nuclear Bombs from Terrorists."

20. Schneider, "Elite U.S. Team Works to Keep Nuclear Bombs from Terrorists."

21. U.S. Department of Energy, "Nuclear Emergency Search Team," http://www.fas.org/nuke/ guide/usa/doctrine/doe/o5530_2. htm (Accessed May 19, 2010).

22. Kenneth Scroggins, "Nuclear Emergency Search Team," Delta Green, http://www.delta-green.com/ opensource/textbook/nest.html (Accessed December 14, 2009).

23. eCharcha.com, "Nuclear Emergency Response," http://www. echarcha.com/forum/archive/ index.php/t-10604.html (Accessed June 23, 2010).

Bibliography

Birchall, Peter. *The Longest Walk: The World of Bomb Disposal.* New York: Sterling, 1998.

Brodie, Thomas G. *Bombs and Bombing: A Handbook to Protection, Security, Disposal, and Investigation for Industry, Police and Fire Departments.* 3d ed. Springfield, Ill.: Charles C. Thomas, 2005.

Esposito, Richard, and Ted Gerstein. *Bomb Squad: A Year Inside the Nation's Most Exclusive Police Unit.* New York: Hyperion, 2007.

Gurney, Peter. *Braver Men Walk Away.* Seneca, N.Y.: Ulversoft, 1994.

Richelson, Jeffrey. *Defusing Armageddon: Inside NEST, America's Secret Nuclear Bomb Squad.* New York: W.W. Norton, 2009.

Ryder, Chris. *A Special Kind of Courage: Bomb Disposal and the Inside Story of 321 EOD Squadron.* London: Methuen, 2005.

Smith, Gary. *Demo Men: Harrowing True Stories from the Military's Elite Bomb Squads.* New York: Pocket, 1997.

Styles, George. *Bombs Have No Pity: My War Against Terrorism.* London: Luscombe, 1975.

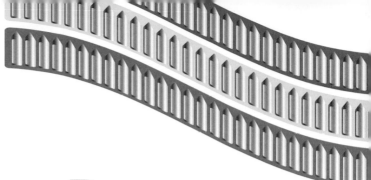

Further Resources

Print

Lenz, Robert. *Explosives and Bomb Disposal Guide.* Sterling, Ill.: Charles C. Thomas, 1976. A guide to explosives and bomb disposal written for law enforcement officers.

Smith, Jim. *A Law Enforcement and Security Officer's Guide to Responding to Bomb Threats: Providing a Working Knowledge of Bombs, Preparing for Such Incidents, and Performing Basic Analysis of Potential Threats.* 2d ed. Springfield, Ill.: Charles C. Thomas, 2009. An instruction manual on evaluating and dealing with bomb threats.

Yinon, Jehuda. *Counterterrorist Detection Techniques of Explosives.* New York. Elsevier Science, 2007. Military/police techniques for detecting explosives.

Online

Bureau of Alcohol, Tobacco, Firearms and Explosives
http://www.atf.gov
Official Web site of the ATF, including its history, descriptions of procedures, and details of major cases.

Department of Defense Explosives Safety Board
http://www.ddesb.pentagon.mil
Official Web site of the Pentagon's primary agency in charge of safe handling of explosives.

The World of Explosives
http://www.explosives.org
Comprehensive information on the history and uses of explosives, safe handling, etc., with a bibliography of other sources.

Index

About the Author

Michael Newton has published 229 books since 1977, with 18 forth-coming from various houses through 2011. His history of the Florida Ku Klux Klan (*The Invisible Empire,* 2001) won the Florida Historical Society's 2002 Rembert Patrick Award for "Best Book in Florida History," and his *Encyclopedia of Cryptozoology* was one of the American Library Association's Outstanding Reference Works in 2006. His non-fiction work includes numerous volumes for Chelsea House Publishers and Facts on File.